invite
PRESS

COME ALIVE:

Conversations with Scripture

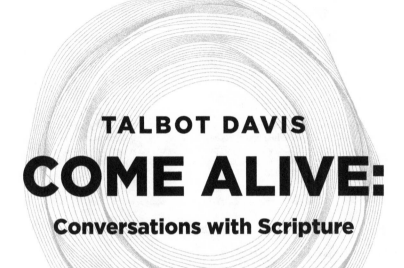

TALBOT DAVIS
COME ALIVE:
Conversations with Scripture

Galatians and Ephesians

**invite
PRESS**

Plano, Texas

To Taylor & Nate, Riley & Natalie. In a book about epistles, you all make these words of Scripture come alive for us:

"You yourselves are all the endorsement we need. Your very lives are a letter that anyone can read by just looking at you"
(2 Corinthians 3:2, MSG).

Introduction
to Paul's Letters

T he New Testament letters in general, and Paul's letters in particular, cannot be authentically or properly read without first revealing two important truths:

Truth #1: No New Testament letter was written to you.
Not one.

Truth #2: No New Testament letter was written to be read in solitude or in silence. Nope, not one.

I firmly believe that not only will coming to grips with these truths help you make more sense of Paul's epistolary treasures, but when you read them on their terms (rather than yours), Paul's words will truly come alive to you.

Let's first look at Truth #1: *No New Testament letter was written to you.*

Paul's letters—and the rest of the biblical library, for that matter—have an original audience who needed to hear his original message. Paul wrote Ephesians to the church in the city of Ephesus, and he wrote Galatians to the churches in the region of Galatia. Although the letters were written to these early first-century churches, they were later lovingly and supernaturally preserved for you.

When you understand that truth, you'll never ask the most pointless question in the history of Bible study: "What does this mean to me?" Guess what? It doesn't matter what it means to you. Bible study is the thrilling process of discerning what it meant to *the original audience,* and then seeing how that meaning intersects with our lives today. This process doesn't make the Bible less relevant; it makes it exponentially more relevant. By excavating what Paul had to say to real churches made up of real people going through real drama in real time, you are better able to celebrate the message's enduring impact on your life and mine.

Now for Truth #2: *No New Testament letter was written to be read in solitude or in silence.*

Most of us are conditioned to open our Bibles (either the old-fashioned kind that looks like a book or the newfangled apps on our phones), turn on a reading light, and read the Word of God silently and meditatively. This *Come Alive* series will help you do that. However, we must always keep in mind that in their original design, these letters were written to be *heard* and not simply *read*.

Literacy rates were extraordinarily low in ancient times, and author Paul envisioned that his letters would have a designated reader who would share the contents out loud in a public commemoration with a gathered, listening congregation.

Now you know why Paul told the Romans, "Faith comes from hearing" (Romans 10:17), when for many of us it has come through reading. You also have clarity as to why Colossians concludes with this instruction: "After this letter *has been read to you*, see that it is also read in the church of the Laodiceans" (4:16, emphasis added).

Understanding how the early church used these letters makes all the difference in both interpretation and application. As you go through the pages of this volume of *Come Alive*, you'll not only learn how Paul's letters were written for the ear more than for the eye, but how our author composed them with a playwright's flair. Much of Ephesians, like Romans before it, lends itself not only to public reading but to public performing. Paul deliberately wrote his letters in a manner that enabled his listeners to both hear and experience them. Because of this, Paul's letters have the capacity to do much more than help prove theological points; they can dynamically help shape and impact lives.

I pray that this volume of the *Come Alive* series will help you love the Scriptures so that you can adore the Savior.

Who Were the Galatians?

Galatians is unique among Paul's letters in that he did not write it to a single church (like the church at Rome or the church at Philippi) or to an individual (as with 1 and 2 Timothy) but to a collection of churches within the region of Galatia, a rugged area in what is today southwestern Turkey.

If it's true that all New Testament letters were written to real people going through real drama in real time, then who were the Galatian people, what was their drama, and when did it all happen?

The Galatians were a Gentile people who had come to faith in Christ from the pagan religions that dotted the landscape of Asia Minor. As Gentiles, they were steeped neither in the way of Moses nor in the customs of the synagogue. Their naivete toward all things Hebrew became one of the great ironies of Paul's letter and the occasion of its writing.

What was their drama? To set that stage, you need to know that the Galatian churches were the only congregations Paul ever addressed with this kind of invective: *"You foolish Galatians! Who has bewitched you?"* (Galatians 3:1). Apparently soul saving was more important to Paul than friend making! Suffice it to say that the Galatian drama involved several false teachers who had slipped into the churches' congregations and sown both confusion and discord. I look forward to spelling out this drama with you in the forthcoming pages, as we look at the parallels between what happened in AD 50 and what continues to occur today in the 2020s.

What About Ephesians?

Unlike Galatia, the church in Ephesus was a singular congregation in a cosmopolitan city. The city of Ephesus was located on the western coast of Turkey on the Aegean Sea. You can visit the remaining ruins of the city on any excursion to that region of the world. Like Galatia, the people in the Ephesian church were primarily Gentile. Their drama differed slightly from their neighbors' in that it involved merging Jews and Gentiles together within the same congregation. How could God make something new and different out of two people so separate and distinct?

Ephesians makes more sense as a letter when you read Acts 19 and see what happened when Paul established a ministry there. Paul arrived, he baptized nascent converts, he grew the church, he threatened the idol-making industry, and he got run out of town in a violent riot. It's a thrilling chapter that helps inform this engaging letter.

Internal evidence suggests that Ephesians was written to be *performed* as much as *read.* We know that Paul was a missionary, pastor, evangelist, and essayist. Is it possible that he was a playwright as well? I believe Ephesians 1 will provide the answer.

What a privilege it is to serve as your guide! With that, I hope that the New Testament letters will *come alive* to you and in you as you read this volume.

This map will help you picture the location of the region of Galatia and the city of Ephesus. The region is now part of modern-day Turkey. When we say "Context Is Everything," that means geography as well!

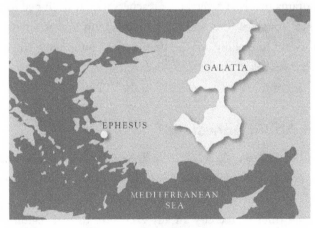

DAY ONE
Galatians 1:1–10

This letter of Paul's is not as lengthy as Paul's magnum opus—Romans—or his fiery personal defense of 1 and 2 Corinthians, but it packs a theological and pastoral punch nonetheless. Here are a few notes about Paul's letters to churches that you may not be aware of; they will be helpful to keep at the forefront of your mind:

1. Each letter addresses a real church in real time dealing with real people living in real situations. They are not treatises or term papers or essays. They were typically forged in conflict and targeted toward resolution.

2. We tend to read them as if they are examples of *modern American letter writing*. They are instead examples of *ancient Greek speechmaking*. They were written to be *heard out loud and in community* rather than *read in silence and in private*.

3. Paul did not sit down with a pen and paper and "write" the letters. Instead, he dictated them to a scribe, who took down what he wrote on ancient papyrus. We see this in living color in Romans 16:22: "I, Tertius, who wrote down this letter, greet you in the Lord." The "dictated" nature of Paul's letters explains some of his stops, starts, and "oh, by the way" moments.

4. The million-dollar question is this: Did Paul or his scribes *know* they were writing inspired scripture? I am not certain. What I am sure about, however, is that the result is in fact *inspired, eternal, and true.*

As we start Galatians, here are the who, what, when, where, and why for this letter:

Who: Unlike Rome, Corinth, and Philippi, whom Paul also wrote and oversaw, Galatia was not a city. Instead, it was a region in what we today call Turkey. Paul had founded these Galatian churches and knew the people, which explains the personal and passionate tone of his words.

What: As already stated, this was a dictated letter from Paul, recorded by a scribe, to a collection of churches. Paul authored this letter assuming it would be read out loud in one church and then passed on to the next.

When: Best estimates range from AD 49 to 54.

Where: Unlike 2 Timothy or Philippians, Galatians is not a prison letter, as Paul had yet to be arrested for the crime of being a Christian. Many experts believe that he wrote this letter to the Galatians shortly after returning from his earliest missionary journey, a hypothesis that answers the "when" question.

Why: In Galatia, we'll see some of Paul's most incendiary rhetoric. Paul has heard news that the Galatian churches have been infiltrated with false teachers—Judaizers, they were called—and that as a result, the churches had begun to practice a different gospel altogether.

With that, let's start by reading Galatians 1:1–10. I encourage you to read it out loud first, as that was Paul's original design.

Notice that from Galatians 1:1, Paul asserts his authority and his position as "Paul, an apostle." Because Paul did not walk with or know Jesus during the Savior's time on earth, his opponents in the church often suggested that he did not have the same clout as Peter, James, John, and the rest of the original apostles. These attacks were particularly acute in Galatia and Corinth. Paul's defense is immediate and emphatic, as not only does he assert his apostleship, but he goes on to say that he was "sent not by men nor by a man, but by

Jesus Christ and God the Father, who raised him from the dead" (1:1). In other words, "I have resurrection connections, so you'd best listen to what I say!"

Paul's "coauthors" are "all the brothers and sisters with me" (1:2). In other words, he includes in his authorship not only the scribe for this letter but all of the fellow evangelists and church planters with whom he regularly travels.

Paul's address "to the churches in Galatia" (1:2b) indicates that this is a regional letter.

Paul's first wish for these churches was "grace and peace" (1:3); meaning, love and favor you do not deserve (grace), leading to a life of serenity you cannot achieve (peace). Paul located the source of grace and peace in "God our Father and the Lord Jesus Christ, who gave himself for our sins to rescue us from the present evil . . . to whom be glory for ever and ever" (1:4–5). This is a pleasant opening. It's also the calm before the storm. The storm hits with both urgency and ferocity in the next couple of verses:

> I am astonished that you are so quickly deserting the one who called you to live in the grace of Christ and are turning to a different gospel—which is really no gospel at all. (1:6–7a)

In this abrupt and aggressive shift, you see that Paul knows the Galatian people well—well enough to scold them without much prelude—and that he believes that the gospel must be both preserved and defended with vigor.

What is the source of this "different gospel"? "Evidently some people are throwing you into confusion and are trying to pervert the gospel of Christ," he says (1:7b). False teachers have infiltrated the Galatian churches, spreading religious misinformation and theological lies. What is the nature of this misinformation? Galatians 1:6 provides a foreshadow: "You are . . . deserting the one who called you to live in the grace of Christ." The perversion of the gospel has to do with the subversion of grace.

How does Paul feel about the false teachers? Galatians 1:8 tells us once, and in case we didn't catch it the first time, Paul repeats his admonition in verse 9: "Let them be under God's curse!"

What could be so serious? Exactly how did the twisting of the gospel lead to Paul's rage? How will he recover his balance in this letter to friends? We will find out in the next section of his letter.

....

**Any perversion of the gospel begins with a
subversion of grace.**

....

DAY TWO
Galatians 1:11-24

Grace is not always comforting. There are times when it needs to challenge you and stretch you. Yet God's grace is *always amazing*. Galatians will reveal that to us time after time.

When we left Paul and the Galatians yesterday, the apostle had just begun his letter by admonishing—nearly insulting—his recipients: "I am astonished that you are so quickly deserting the one who called you to live in the grace of Christ" (1:6).

One time I received a note from a friend from Good Shepherd Church who shared this memory: "Years ago in our Sunday school classes at my home, one of the teachers began her lesson with this remark: 'If I had been Paul writing this letter to these churches, I would have begun with "Dear Idiots of Galatia!" We all howled with laughter, but Paul's accusation feels true.'

Many of us are swayed by every wind of doctrine that comes along, falling victim to the notion that newer must be better, and younger has to be smarter. I can only imagine Paul's level of frustration as he recalled his time mentoring the Galatian Christians, only to learn they had "fallen away" (see Galatians 5:4). Paul feels compelled to remind the Galatians in this part of his letter that the gospel is for treasuring, not modifying.

So, let's look at where Paul goes next in addressing the "Idiots of Galatia"! As we do so, remember this: Not only is the gospel under attack in those churches, but so is Paul's own claim to apostolic authority. That's why his story turns autobiographical.

In Galatians 1:11–12 Paul defends his authority:

> I want you to know, brothers and sisters, that the gospel I preached is not of human origin. I did not receive it from any man, nor was I taught it; rather, I received it by revelation from Jesus Christ.

How glorious is that?! Paul refers here to his conversion and its immediate aftermath, a story that Luke chronicles with remarkable detail in Acts 9. Paul's words regarding the divine origin of the gospel remind me of the lyrics to Rich Mullins's song "Creed," in which he says that it is what he *believes* that makes him who he is. He goes on to say:

> I did not make it, no it is making me.
> It is the very truth of God and not the invention of any man.
> (Rich Mullins, "Creed," by Mullins, in *A Liturgy, a Legacy, & a Ragamuffin Band*, Reunion, 1993, studio album.)

"The very truth of God is not the invention of any man," Mullins says. I find that liberating. Any faith we invent becomes all about us, but the faith we inherit is all about God. The gospel is an improbable invasion of history by our incomparable God. The gospel is not history that the church somehow *made up*. It is instead history that continues to *make us*.

In Galatians 1:13–16, Paul gives us the "*Reader's Digest* Condensed Version" of his upbringing, accomplishments, and conversion. Notice the reference in 1:14 to his advancement within Judaism's institutional hierarchy, as well as his zealousness for its traditions. Paul rarely missed an opportunity to mention his achievements both against and for Jesus. In verse 15, everything changes, as Paul says: "But . . . God . . ."

Two of the most significant words in human language are "but God." I know in my own case, I was headed for a life of hollow cynicism and futile striving, *but God* intervened with saving grace. You likely have a *but God* moment in your life as well. Maybe several.

You'd be bound for hell . . . *but God* . . .

You'd be isolated from others in your narcissism . . . *but God* . . .

You'd be in jail . . . *but God* . . .

You'd be in and out of rehab . . . *but God* . . .

You'd be in permanent despair . . . *but God* . . .

You'd never be good enough in the eyes of your parents, peers, or yourself . . . *but God* . . .

You'd live life without certainty of your place in eternity . . . *but God* . . .

Notice Paul's belief about this God who interrupts our lives, forcefully if he must: "But when God, who set me apart from my mother's womb and called me by his grace . . ." (1:15). Paul saw the direction of his life as so unexpected, so unlikely, so miraculous, that it had to be planned from the moment of his conception. If you are a Christian, and that faith is more in spite of your upbringing than because of it, you know well what Paul is talking about.

Paul winds up Galatians 1 by discussing his post-conversion travels. First, he went to Arabia (1:17a), suggesting that he spent time alone in the desert, listening to God and gaining further revelation into the gospel.

He next traveled to Damascus (1:17b), the very city where he was traveling to arrest and persecute Christians when he had his *but God* moment in Acts 9! Paul apparently stayed there three years, long enough to get his "master of divinity" at "Damascus Theological Seminary" if he studied full-time.

After those three years, he ventured down to Jerusalem (1:18) to meet with Cephas: that is, Peter. We'll see in Galatians 2:11 that the clash of those two particular egos came with its own ecclesiastical drama. Paul spent fifteen days with Peter in Jerusalem and while there met Jesus' brother James (1:19). Talk about a fly-on-the-wall wish! What did these titans of faith talk about, and how did they get along? We may never know for sure.

Finally, Paul traveled to "Syria and Cilicia" (1:21) near the region of Tarsus . . . Paul's way of saying, "I returned to the place where

I grew up." His arrival was no doubt unsettling to many of the Christians and churches, as his reputation as a persecutor and accessory to murder (see Acts 7) preceded him. Yet his *but God* run of blessing and favor continued: "And they praised God because of me" (1:24).

What came next in his journey of faith? How did Paul arrive at his place of influence in the church? And how does all that relate to the "idiocy" of the Galatians in embracing "another gospel"? For answers to those questions and more, we will move on to the next chapter of Paul's famous letter.

Today is a great day to recall three of your most vivid "but God" moments. As you remember them, pause, and give the Lord thanks for his amazing grace.

DAY THREE
Galatians 2:1-10

....

In yesterday's reading, Paul granted us a remarkable window into his autobiography:

Paul was advanced in Judaism.
He was chosen from his mother's womb.
He was spending his life persecuting the church with great fervor.

"But God" intervened.

Early Christians converted and then discipled Paul in both Arabia and Damascus.
Paul traveled to Jerusalem to bond with Peter.

There, Paul had a sort of homecoming and received a welcome from the very believers he had previously persecuted.

In today's section of Paul's Letter to the Galatians (2:1–10), the memoir continues.

Galatians 2:1 looks innocent enough but is loaded with intrigue:

Then after fourteen years, I went up again to Jerusalem, this time with Barnabas. I took Titus along also.

What had Paul been doing for fourteen years? He was embarking on missionary trips around the Mediterranean world, as the book of Acts tells us! When Paul said he went "up" to Jerusalem (1:18), he was referring to altitude and not to going north on the map. The Songs of Ascent (Psalms 120–134) were given that name for that very same reason, as the pilgrims sang them as they trudged *up* the hills to Jerusalem for religious festivals.

Back to 2:1. Why would I say it was "loaded with intrigue"? Because of this small detail: "I took Titus along also." Titus—the same

Titus who received an "inspired, eternal, and true" letter from Paul that made it into the New Testament—was Gentile, not Jewish. He was uncircumcised. He ate pork and shellfish. He didn't observe the Jewish holidays. He wouldn't have known the Songs of Ascent. Paul brought Titus to the citadel of Judaism, the city of Jerusalem. By the way, the majority of the Galatians' first readers and hearers were themselves Gentiles.

Notice in verse 2:2 how Paul meets with the long-established leaders of the Jerusalem church with an attitude of humility: "I wanted to be sure I was not running and had not been running my race in vain." In other words, he wanted to ensure that his message was correct and that his methods were appropriate. He placed himself under the authority of the Jerusalem apostles. While there, he received the good news that his traveling companion, Titus, did not have to endure circumcision to keep the peace.

Why was this even an issue? Galatians 2:4 tells us: "This matter arose because some false believers had infiltrated our ranks to spy on the freedom we have in Christ Jesus and to make us slaves." At this moment, the feel of the letter turns, and Paul's autobiographical tone becomes adversarial. These same false teachers had infiltrated the Galatian churches – a point Paul will make with great ferocity ahead in chapter 3. The content of the false teaching was as follows: to be *Christian*, you first have to become *Jewish*. Men have to receive circumcision, and both genders must follow kosher food laws and observe Jewish rituals and festivals. Paul—himself still an observant Jew—regarded this burden as "slavery."

I love Galatians 2:5, where we see Paul's resolve: "We did not give in to them for a moment." Notice too his protective attitude for the gospel: "so that the truth of the gospel might be preserved for you."

Galatians 2:6–10 goes on to record how the leaders of the Jerusalem church were in one accord regarding Titus in particular and the Gentiles in general. In fact, Peter, James, and John agreed with Paul regarding his unique mission of gospel proclamation to Gentile populations—an assignment that mirrored Peter's own with Jewish populations.

These two titans—Peter and Paul—presented the same gospel to disparate people groups. The only molding the gospel received was in *method*, not in *content*. Although Paul may have been tempted to have Titus and others circumcised to "keep the peace," church leadership agreed that such compromise was not necessary. As Acts 4:12 has already told us, "salvation is found in no one else, for there is no other name under heaven given to mankind by which we must be saved." It's not Jesus *plus* Moses. It's not Christ *and* Judaism. It's in Christ alone.

What Paul says here in Galatians lines up completely with the decision the larger church reached in the Jerusalem Council, which Luke describes in Acts 15. That particular council—much like the first "Annual Conference" or "General Synod" meeting in church history—had debated this same topic: "Do Gentiles have to become Jewish before they can become Christian?" The ultimate answer?

> We should not make it difficult for the Gentiles who are turning to God. Instead we should write to them, telling them to abstain from food polluted by idols, from sexual immorality, from the meat of strangled animals, and from blood (Acts 15:19–20).

The church had made its decision and could move on to the next conversation. Supposedly, that is.

While it may seem like an insignificant matter to us today, this was the primary dilemma of the early church: *Will we remain a particular expression of Judaism? Or will we become a global movement of the kind that Jesus envisioned in Matthew 28?*

At this stage, the answer seems settled. As long as Paul and his cohorts "remember[ed] the poor" (Galatians 2:10) while proclaiming the gospel, they were free to bring a message of freedom to the uncircumcised. So far, so good, at least in theory.

However, when theory met practice and when this idea collided with reality, trouble ensued. To see what I mean by that, tune in next for the "Clash of the Theological Titans."

....

We don't sing "In Christ Among." We sing "In Christ Alone."

....

DAY FOUR
Galatians 2:11–21

Who knew it could be possible to turn a personal confrontation into gospel proclamation? Stay with me in Galatians 2, and you'll see exactly how that happens. This section is perhaps my favorite in the entire Galatian letter. I say that because it begins with a genuine *mano a mano smackdown* between two giants of the early church and then leads to the greatest truth of the Christian gospel. What could be better?

When you have two pillars of *anything* and they have a falling-out, it's must-see TV. It's like Rodgers and Hammerstein, Simon & Garfunkel, Lennon–McCartney, Peaches & Herb, a Tupac and Biggie–level fallout. In this case it's Peter and Paul. As in Saint Peter and Saint Paul. The first pope (Peter) and the author of a large chunk of the New Testament (Paul). Alpha male and, well, alpha male. Sometimes when you have two egos and two personalities of that size and influence, it can suck the rest of the air out of the room, which is probably what happened when they ran into each other at a church covered dish supper in Antioch. Add to all that the world's most vexing religious question of that day and look what happens in Galatians 2:11:

> When Cephas came to Antioch, I opposed him to his face, because he stood condemned.

Whoa! Public rebuke! The kind I'd be reluctant to do. I am much more likely to sidle up to someone and say, "Can we talk about this in my office, please?" But Paul took it public, and that's probably because the nature of the thing Peter had done was so pernicious. Look at 2:12–13:

For before certain men came from James, he used to eat with the Gentiles. But when they arrived, he began to draw back and separate himself from the Gentiles because he was afraid of those who belonged to the circumcision group. The other Jews joined him in his hypocrisy, so that by their hypocrisy even Barnabas was led astray.

Oh no! Not Barney! So, here's what's going on: two groups of people, Jews and Gentiles, had long been separated by race, diet, religion, and custom. Yet now these two, who had previously kept more than their distance from each other, were in the church, together. Peter, a Jew himself, had earlier been instrumental in breaking down Jew–Gentile walls, as recorded in Acts 10 when he received a word from God that all food was now clean, not just that which is kosher.

However, when "men . . . from James," a group of influential Jews—including Jesus' own brother—from down in Jerusalem trekked up to Antioch to check out the sound system in the "happening church" there, Peter reverted. Less emphasis here on what he ate than on who he was comfortable eating with. Perhaps there was social pressure, perhaps ethnic guilt, or perhaps simply a desire to get along by going along, but Peter repealed what he had written and went back to his old ways. I think I know why: he had been raised from birth to think of himself and fellow Jews as slightly *better than* the Gentiles. Chosen by God? Check. Don't eat pork? Check. Don't worship idols? Check. Better hygiene practices? Check. More self-control? Check. All these tokens of status and responsibility and identity were so hard to give up.

It's so easy to hang on to where you were born and what you've done, and to think that you're just a little better than others because of it. Peter was not really being wicked; just normal.

I know in my case, I tend to look at people, and as an expression of my insecurity, I think, "Well, I'm better dressed, educated, spoken, polished, maybe a better tennis player." I remember a time in fact that I heard a fellow pastor preaching on the radio and refused to be blessed by his sermon. Why? Because I was obsessed with my "better" sermons! Life is full of comparison and competition. I even remember going to a denominational meeting a few years ago, in which our name tags were color coded according to our levels of ordination! Like, Good, Better, Best. It made me think of the Star-Belly Sneetches in Dr. Seuss's masterpiece of separation, division, jealousy, and "better than." (See https://www.google.com/books/edition/The_Sneetches_and_Other_Stories_Read_Lis/Ab04DwAAQBAJ?hl=en&gbpv=1&dq=the+sneetches.) Few things are more dangerous than when the world of "better than" invades the world of faith.

This is what Peter had done. He fell into the "better thans" because of his lifelong religious position as a child of Israel. Here's how Paul describes the problem in 2:14:

> When I saw that they were not acting in line with the truth of the gospel, I said to Cephas in front of them all, "You are a Jew, yet you live like a Gentile and not like a Jew. How is it, then, that you force Gentiles to follow Jewish customs?"

Notice the severity of Paul's rebuke. Peter was not merely acting badly or with social insensitivity; he was perverting the faith. The gospel is the good news of Jesus' life, death, resurrection, reign, and return and how God promises us heaven. Peter's behavior had turned treasure into poison.

Paul went on. What follows is either a blow-by-blow narration of his further conversation with Peter or simply his riff on it; we don't know. Look at 2:15–16:

> We who are Jews by birth and not sinful Gentiles know that a person is not justified by the works of the law, but by faith in Jesus Christ. So we, too, have put our faith in Christ Jesus that we may be justified by faith in Christ and not by the works of the law, because by the works of the law no one will be justified.

We are *made right* with God more than we *get right* with God. By the way, the "works of the law" in these verses doesn't refer to good deeds. It instead means circumcision, kosher laws, temple practices, and anything else that made Jews "better than."

Check out 2:17:

But if, in seeking to be justified in Christ, we Jews find ourselves also among the sinners, doesn't that mean that Christ promotes sin? Absolutely not!

Now, that's funny. Here's what Paul was saying: if Jesus arranges, demands, and creates a church where Jews and Gentiles hang together and eat together, is that sinning? Absolutely not! It may seem like an absurd question, but I remember that time in the early 1990s when a fellow pastor in our town received no small amount of criticism for being in a biracial marriage although the church itself was multiethnic. That criticism always struck me as a combination of backward and ungodly until I heard the same thing happening in the 2010s and the subject of the condemnation was the church I serve in Charlotte, North Carolina! I have never been more delighted to be criticized!

Paul's argument builds in 2:19–21:

For through the law I died to the law so that I might live for God. I have been crucified with Christ and I no longer live, but Christ lives in me. The life I now live in the body, I live by faith in the Son of God, who loved me and gave himself for me. I do not set aside the grace of God, for if righteousness could be gained through the law, Christ died for nothing!

Look at 2:21 again: "I do not set aside the grace of God, for if righteousness could be gained through the law, Christ died for nothing!"

If you rely on "better thans," either consciously or subconsciously, then Jesus wasted his time on the cross. If you are good enough in any way to merit your position among God's saved, the Father played a trick on the Son, a painfully bloody trick; in fact, the worst trick ever. If all religions are basically the same and everyone goes to heaven in the end, then Jesus suffered for nothing. If there's one way for Jews and another way for Gentiles and another way for the wellborn and well-bred, and another way for the Brahmins and another way for the untouchables, then Jesus went through the worst travesty of all time. But none of that is true, not one bit of it. There's no one who has made or will make it due to their birth or their behavior. Paul took a personal confrontation and turned it into gospel proclamation. And in doing so he tells us something masterful: *Heaven's not a reward for those who are better. It's a gift for those who've been bought.* That's the good news.

What Paul was talking about that day—*no more divisions*—is not a result of the gospel. It is the heart of the gospel. I need rescue as much as the pimp, the prostitute, the addict, the imprisoned, the venture capitalist, or the dictator. In fact, the first thing I need rescue from is the sense that I am in any way better than the folks I just mentioned. You don't *get right* with God by being better than other people; you're *made right* with God through your allegiance to Jesus, who is Rescuer and King. The purchase price for all of us is exactly the same! Jesus' blood. The same amount for each one.

Think of a contest in which three men set out in a swimming race from Los Angeles to Honolulu. All are great swimmers with cut bodies and enormous lungs. Yet pretty soon, a few miles in, one of the swimmers just stops, drops off, and sinks into oblivion in the Pacific. Loser. So, we're left with two. A few more miles, a second guy, the same thing. Struggles and then gives up. Loser. The third swimmer realizes, "I win! I'm not only better than; I'm the best!" And one hundred yards later—because he's still got to get to Hawaii—his lungs give out, his arms give way, and he joins his friends at the bottom of the Pacific. One was better, but all are dead. That race is as pointless as it is at any level to try to trust in your betterness. You might be better at some things. But God is not grading on a curve. He's grading on the cross.

It is better to trust in your incompleteness and your ineptitude, because this is what will drive you to appreciate grace. I hope for all of you that your awareness of your own helplessness will be ever increasing, so that your appreciation of Jesus' grace may be ever deepening.

Who is that "other person" for you? Is it the immigrant? The smelly? The rich? The entitled? The Democrat? The Republican? The smoker? Today is a great day to relinquish every "better than" you possess to the control of the One who has bought us all.

Heaven's not a reward for those who are better.
It's a gift for those who've been bought.

DAY FIVE
Galatians 3:1-14

....

In yesterday's reading, Galatians 2:11–21, we saw how Paul confronted Peter over his "backsliding" into a works-based, Jewish-focused Christian faith. Today, if you can imagine, he turns the heat up as he confronts the Galatians themselves.

Paul begins with these startling words: "You foolish Galatians!" (3:1). You get the sense that Paul has been suppressing his true feelings up until this moment. Now, he can't hold it in anymore and the truth comes out, unfiltered and unvarnished. He hopes the Galatians will be shocked into action and repentance.

With that opening salvo, Paul questions the source of their faulty beliefs: "Who has bewitched you?" (3:1b). He has already referred to the bewitchers in 1:7: "Evidently some people are throwing you into confusion and are trying to pervert the gospel of Christ." Paul now invites the Galatians to own their vulnerability to the false teaching and their complicity in believing it.

Paul then moves to a series of rhetorical questions. With each one, he knows the answer, and yet he designs them all to awaken the Galatians from their stupor.

Did you receive the Spirit by works of the law or by believing what you heard? (v. 2b)

Are you so foolish? (v. 3a)

After beginning by the means of the Spirit, are you now trying to finish by means of the flesh? (v. 3b)

Have you experienced so much in vain? (v. 4a)

- 19 -

Does God give you his Spirit . . . by works of the law, or by believing
what you heard? (v. 5)

Seldom does Paul string so many consecutive questions together.
Remember that New Testament epistles are more examples of ancient Greek speechmaking than they are of modern American letter
writing. Paul's rhetorical purpose is to expose the absurdity of the
Galatians' regression into a law-based religion, a regression all the
more curious when you realize they weren't Jewish to begin with.

By this stage, Paul hopes the Galatians are looking at each other
wistfully, acknowledging, *"Wow. How quickly we have forgotten the
goodness of God. How silly of us to be saved by faith but then think we
can become mature by law."*

To underscore his point, Paul holds up the example of Abraham, the father of Judaism. By what standard was Abraham counted
as "approved" by God? "He believed the LORD, and he credited it
to him as righteousness," Genesis 15:6 tells us. With that approval
comes an assignment: "All peoples on earth will be blessed through
you" (Genesis 12:3, retweeted here in Galatians 3:8 as "All nations
will be blessed through you"). Abraham was the forerunner of all
who would be saved by faith, and that faith carries with it the global
assignment of spreading the good news to all nations.

In verses 10–14 Paul deploys more shocking language to convey
the same truth. In 3:10–11, he points out that if you're hoping to be
counted worthy before God by your obedience to Mosaic law, even
one transgression of that law will leave you out (v. 10). Given the
impossibility of that task, God gives us the good news: "the righteous
shall live by faith" (v. 11), rephrased from Habakkuk 2:4. If you try
to achieve salvation, you can't receive it. By receiving salvation, you
demonstrate that you actually believe it.

Paul reaches back to his Old Testament arsenal and pulls out
Deuteronomy 21:23: "anyone who is hung on a pole is under God's
curse." He couples that with the most paradoxically beautiful state-

ment in this entire section: Jesus redeemed us "by becoming a curse for us" (Galatians 3:13). In our place, as our sin, embodying the curse we deserve, Jesus really, truly paid it all. Not some. All. How dare we try to add to what Jesus has already done by thinking our salvation depends on our further efforts?

Notice how Paul concludes the section, and pay special attention to the language: "He redeemed us in order that the blessing given to Abraham might come to the Gentiles through Christ Jesus," meaning, that what Israel could not do as a nation, Jesus does as a Messiah, "so that by faith we might receive the promise of the Spirit" (3:14).

Did you see how he ends? Whereas we would likely say "so that by faith we might be saved" or "so that by faith we might go to heaven after we die," Paul's emphasis is different: faith in the Son leads to filling of the Spirit.

We want to die and go to heaven. Paul wants us to live and bring heaven here.

How will the Holy Spirit empower that life? What does that life look like? That topic will feature prominently in the rest of the letter. In the meantime, would you pray this prayer?

Father, fill me today, afresh, anew, and full, with an outpouring of your Holy Spirit. I believe in your Son by faith. Amen.

DAY SIX
GALATIANS 3:15-25

As we look at this section of Paul's letter to the Galatian churches (remembering that Galatia was a region and not a single city, unlike Corinth, Rome, Ephesus, and the rest), recall the crisis behind the epistle in the first place: the Galatians had begun augmenting their faith in the grace of Jesus with trust in the law of Moses. A group of "Judaizers"—false teachers—had infiltrated the Galatian churches and insisted that the believers there become Jewish in order to become Christian. Paul, himself a Jew of great education, distinction, and accomplishment, would not stand for this and must instead stand against it.

With that in mind, today's reading becomes an explanation from history as to the superiority of grace to law. Paul seeks to prove that the era of grace predates the era of the law. I have been reading Galatians a long time and had never paid close attention to these words and Paul's time line until preparing this book, proving that you can always learn from the Word. We're always moving toward maturity yet have never completely achieved it!

This explains Paul's words in Galatians 3:16:

> The promises were spoken to Abraham and to his seed. Scripture does not say "and to seeds," meaning many people, but "and to your seed," meaning one person, who is Christ.

This refers to Genesis 12:7, in the narrative where Abraham received his initial call from God: "The LORD appeared to Abram and said, 'To your offspring I will give this land.'" If your Bible has footnotes, it may well add "or seed" for "offspring." Paul takes all that to mean that the singularity of offspring/seed is an early reference to the coming of Christ. Add to that the basis of Abraham's covenant with God: "Abram believed the LORD, and he credited to him as righteousness" (Genesis 15:6). Abram (later changed to Abraham) responded to God with faith and so became his child as well as the father of the nations. It was not his performance for God that made him "right"; it was his relationship with God that did so.

Paul's point is chronological: Abraham lived some 430 years (Galatians 3:17) before Moses, so the Law that Moses brought from Mount Sinai (the Ten Commandments and all the rest) was by definition a secondary arrangement. Faith came first through Abraham; the Law came second through Moses. The notion that the era of grace predates the era of the Law would have been revolutionary to both the "Judaizing" teachers and their gullible students in Galatia.

After establishing that grace was first, Paul then asked a logical question: "Why, then, was the law given at all?" (Galatians 3:19a). He gives two primary reasons:

1. To raise awareness of sin (3:19b, 3:22). If we didn't have laws such as "Thou shalt not covet," or "Honor thy father and mother," we wouldn't be aware of all the ways we don't keep the law. At least part of the reason for the revealed law is to drive us to grace! "I could never keep all these laws perfectly; I need someone to do it for me!" That's when God says, "Now I have you exactly where I want you. Can I introduce you to my Son?"

2. Galatians 3:24 refers to the law as "our guardian until Christ came." The wording there refers to a particular role that certain individuals had in the ancient world: they would escort children to and from school. These guardians were not teachers; they were instead guides, delivering young boys to their tutors (girls rarely received education in ancient Galatia). Paul says that was the function of Moses' law: to guide us to the place where we could learn from Christ. As a result, "now that this faith has come, we are no longer under a guardian" (3:25).

Paul has punctured the arguments of the Judaizers by appealing to history and to logic. He has used their own weapons against them! We here see Paul at his most Pauline.

When we pick up tomorrow, Paul might just puncture some of our most treasured phrases and naïve beliefs. What could those be? How will Paul unsettle us?

God has us exactly where he wants us when we become aware of our sin. That's when God steps in and asks, "Have you met my Son?"

DAY SEVEN
Galatians 3:26-4:7

....

Yesterday, we learned that Abraham's "grace" preceded Moses' "law" and that the function of the law was to serve as our guardian until the era of grace and faith reached its culmination in Jesus. Remember that Paul arranged his argument and made his points so that the Galatian Christians would cease their efforts to become Jewish as an essential part of being Christian. This is another one of those letters that is not written to us but has been preserved for us.

Part of what has been preserved for us is the shock of what comes next, in Galatians 3:26–27. Before I tell you the source of the shock, I want you to consider this very common phrase in modern American culture: *We're all children of God.*

Our parents said it. Politicians say it. Teachers say it. Tweeters tweet it. Facebookers post it. Pastors insist it. Denominational executives declare it. It is usually uttered as the clinching point of any possible argument on a wide array of topics: "Well, we are all children of God after all!"

No. We're not.

What? How could I assert something so . . . hateful?

Because I want to be biblical. And language *matters*. Sloppy language leads to careless theology, which inevitably causes heresy.

Look at Galatians 3:26–27 (emphasis added):

> So *in Christ Jesus* you are all children of God *through faith*, for all of you who were baptized into Christ have clothed yourself with Christ.

Paul's readers were children of God through faith. Not by birth. Not by heritage. Not by accident. By faith, faith in Christ, who then clothes us with himself.

All people are loved by God. Chased by God. Pursued by God. Adored by God. All people, no exceptions. Yet only those who say yes to Jesus become children of God. There's an enormous difference in that statement.

The great enemy of the church is sloppy, sentimental thinking—the kind of thinking Paul went to such lengths to prevent.

Perhaps you are thinking, in response to these two verses, *I never noticed that!* Maybe you're even saying, *"Grrrr! I don't believe it!"* If the latter is the case, know that I'm simply observing what the inspired scripture says and relating it to you. I hope I am doing so in a way that elevates the way you think and speak about this Christ into whom we have been baptized.

Where will Paul go after destroying one of our most cherished American phrases? His words to this point are the prelude for Galatians 3:28:

> There is neither Jew nor Gentile, neither slave nor free, nor is there male and female, for you are all one in Christ Jesus.

What a glorious description of how the ground really is level at the foot of the cross. In our modern world, just think of all the applications. As long as we remember that our "oneness" is not so much in our common humanity as in our shared Savior, there is no longer Asian or Anglo or African or Latino or Red State or Blue State or First World or Global South, for in Christ we are all one. Paul's next words make it clear: "If you belong to Christ, then you are Abraham's seed, and heirs according to the promise." Think of how comprehensive "belonging to Christ" must be! It's not that we merely "believe in Christ" or simply become "acquainted with Christ," but we belong to him. He has complete ownership of us—of our bodies, minds, souls, wallets, and relationships. We belong to one another as we first belong to Christ.

After all that, Paul spends Galatians 4:1–7 making another analogy. Before Christ's coming, we were enslaved "under the elemental spiritual forces of the world" (4:3). Perhaps you know exactly what that's like and the heavy toll such slavery exacted upon you and your family. Then Paul introduces his understanding of the Christmas story:

> But when the set time had fully come, God sent his Son, born of a woman, born under the law, to redeem those under the law, that we might receive adoption to sonship. (4:4–5)

In other words, God became one of us because he adores all of us. That's such great news.

God longs to graft us into his family via adoption, an adoption that is ours not by obeying the law but by exercising faith, not by our performance for Christ but by our position in him.

Paul ends this section where he began (meaning this is an "inclusio"—a literary bookend) with these words: "So you are no longer a slave but God's child [Notice that? There was a time when you weren't his child!]; and since you are his child, God has made you also an heir" (4:7). What we have is a rhetorical and theological tour de force, as every Galatian pretension has been obliterated by the clarity of Paul's words.

Sloppy language leads to careless theology, which inevitably causes heresy.

DAY EIGHT
Galatians 4:8-20

....

If yesterday we saw Paul give a theological tour de force, in today's reading he issues an intensely *personal* appeal to the Galatians.

Paul begins this portion of today's letter (4:8) with a reference to the Galatians' previous lives as pagan polytheists: "Formerly, when you did not know God, you were slaves to those who by nature are not gods." The ancients knew these gods by names, such as Baal, Molech, Zeus, and Athena; I suspect we'd use terms like Facebook, Amazon, and Apple to describe forces that hold us in similar sway today. Paul moves on in 4:9:

> But now that you know God—or rather are known by God—how
> is it that you are turning back to those weak and miserable forces?

In that self-correction we see Paul's dictation at work. He's likely pacing, caught up in his argument, "thinking out loud," and as the words spill out, he realizes that he's captured a half-truth and needs to deliver the truth of our relationship with God: we are "known by God." In 1 Corinthians 1:14–16, we see the same sort of dynamic at work:

> I thank God that I did not baptize any of you except Crispus and
> Gaius, so no one can say that you were baptized in my name. (Yes,
> I also baptized the household of Stephanas; beyond that, I don't
> remember if I baptized anyone else.)

The Bible is so much more enjoyable when you not only know the stories behind the stories but you can also visualize and appreciate the process by which its authors wrote their books.

Back to the content. What does Paul mean by "weak and miserable forces"? How have such forces enslaved the Galatians all over again? Paul makes two daring assertions at once:

1. The Galatians' flirtations with Jewish rituals is a reversion to their pagan idolatry! Galatians 4:8 depicts their idol-worshiping phase; then 4:9–10 suggests that this phase of Judaized faith is the same sort of practice, with the same disastrous consequences as before.

2. The "Judaized" version of Christianity that the Galatians embrace is "weak and miserable" because it can diagnose sin but provides no relief from it. That's what law always does. It points out what's wrong in your life without providing the power of grace to help you overcome it.

Paul then moves to the personal in his appeal. Galatians 4:12 sounds odd, even arrogant, to our ears:

I plead with you, brothers and sisters, become like me, for I became like you.

Remember that Paul was Jewish. Galatia, located in modern-day Turkey, was Gentile. So, when Paul visited them to plant the churches in that region, he adopted Gentile ways to reach Gentile people. He now invites them to return the favor and become grace-centric, as he is.

Paul's next words have stirred up no small amount of speculation. He refers to the illness that he bore when visiting them (4:13), adds that it was a "trial" for them (4:14), and ultimately suggests that his hosts would have "torn out [their] eyes and given them to [him]" (4:15). Does this mean he had an eye ailment? An elongated episode of pink eye? Or could it have been even more serious, such as epilepsy? The heartbreak of psoriasis? Malaria and the often-debilitating headaches with which it afflicts those who have it? We know from 2 Corinthians 10:10 that the Corinthian people found Paul physically unimpressive. Did the Galatians find him somehow repulsive? We don't know any of these answers for certain. What we are sure about, however, is that they have given New Testament scholars many years' worth of employment as they have tried to figure them out!

Paul's point in all this seems to be this: "We have history. I am trustworthy. I long for your best. Reject these Johnny-come-lately Judaizers and return to your first love, Jesus, through your first pastor, me."

His final words of this section (4:17–20) insist that the false teachers who have infiltrated the Galatian churches have ill intent. In contrast, Paul's great longing is that "Christ is formed in you" (4:19). Galatian faith is apparently embryonic, and our apostle longs for them to move to maturity. As I read Paul's words, I wrote a simple, repetitive prayer:

> **Form Christ in me, Lord.**
> **Form Christ in me.**
> **Form Christ in me.**
> **'Perhaps you will pray this prayer with me today.'**

DAY NINE
Galatians 4:21-31

Today's reading is a strange section of the letter made all the stranger by the analogy that Paul draws. Nevertheless, as we persevere through these "stranger things," we'll find some nuggets of gold for life in the twenty-first century.

Paul has just concluded a theological tour de force (3:26–4:7) followed by a passionately personal appeal (4:8–20), all designed to get the Galatian churches to jettison the Judaizing teachers who have infiltrated them and instead return to Paul's grace-centric model and faith-focused teaching.

In today's section, Paul adopts the rather curious strategy of citing an obscure Old Testament story to buttress his point. Why do I call that strategy curious? Because his Galatian audience is Gentile and much more likely to be familiar with the folklore of pagan gods and goddesses than the sacred history of Israel.

Look at his beginning: "Tell me, you who want to be under the law, are you not aware of what the law says?" (4:21). A legitimate answer would be "Not really! We didn't grow up with it; we didn't go through bar mitzvah, like you did, Rabbi Paul, and we're only familiar with what these infiltrating teachers have told us." Yet Paul passes right over the legitimate answer and proceeds to address his own question with a recounting of the rather sordid tale of Abraham, Sarah, Hagar, Isaac, and Ishmael. The broad contours of the story are in Genesis 16–21 and go like this:

Abraham was promised that all the nations of earth would be blessed through his seed.

Abraham and Sarah were barren, a great curse in ancient times and something with which many wrestle to this day.

Abraham and Sarah were also old. The prospects of the promise coming true seemed remote indeed.

Sarah decided to take matters into her own hands and directed Abraham to have sex with her servant girl, Hagar, and thus be able to continue his genealogical line through her.

The plan worked, and Hagar gave birth to Ishmael.

Relational mayhem ensued.

God came through and Sarah gave birth to Isaac.

More relational mayhem ensued, this time spurred on by jealousy and intrigue.

Abraham and Sarah sent Hagar and Ishmael away.

Modern Arabs and many Muslims often trace their ancestry through Ishmael's line. That's why Abraham is the father of the world's three great monotheistic religions: Christianity, Judaism, and Islam.

That's the story as Genesis tells it and as Paul received it.

However, note what Paul says in Galatians 4:24: "These things are being taken figuratively."

They weren't told figuratively. They were told historically. Paul is reaching back and recasting the story to reinforce his theological and pastoral point, which is his right. It was also a relatively common way ancient rabbis read even more ancient stories.

How does this family soap opera involving Abraham and the women who love him relate to law and grace? Here's how:

Ishmael was born of mere human impulses and thus was a child of "slavery." If you trust in yourself and depend on your own performance, that's what you get: slavery to sin and slavery to an impossible standard.

Isaac was born of a promise and thus was a child of "grace." For you, then, "Isaac" comes when you believe in God to do the unbelievable and when you trust God to perform the impossible. Isaac's birth shows that when you don't take things into your own hands that belong in God's hands, the outcome is more glorious than you expect. Is it any wonder that Isaac's name literally means "laughter"?

Notice how Paul summarizes his entire point: "But what does Scripture say? 'Get rid of the slave woman and her son, for the slave woman's son will never share in the inheritance with the free woman's son.'" Yes, Scripture says that—but these are not the words of God but of Sarah! It doesn't mean they're not true; it simply means this is not a "thus saith the Lord" moment. Paul's final word on the matter is in 4:31:

> Therefore, brothers and sisters, we are not children of the slave woman, but of the free woman.

Amen to that.

Where does that freedom lead us? How will an examination of that freedom lead to some of the most shocking and even offensive things Paul ever said? We'll find out in the next section of Paul's letter to the Galatian churches.

Laughter comes when you believe in God to do the unbelievable and trust God to perform the impossible.

DAY TEN
Galatians 5:1-15

How do you grow in faith? Gradually and then suddenly. Adopting a routine of starting the day reading the Scriptures sometimes may feel like a chore and as if you're not really making progress. But then one day, you realize you're thinking biblically. Scripture—not your self-talk—forms your personal outlook. Faith—not what you saw on TMZ—shapes how you feel about cultural issues. And best of all, your nights are filled with serenity and peace because your mornings have been soaked in truth. This signals spiritual growth. As you continue to read through this volume, ask God to grow you "gradually and then suddenly," trusting that God, through Paul, will help you get there.

Paul is relentless. He is not going to veer from his primary point: the Galatians need to stop listening to the false teachers who have infected their churches with a false gospel of "You must become fully Jewish to be authentically Christian" and instead embrace Jesus' gospel of grace. Paul will circle back around to that main point and then punctuate it with some of the most shocking and potentially offensive language in any of his letters. Hold on to your seat!

He begins with a restatement of his overarching thesis:

> It is for freedom that Christ has set us free. Stand firm, then, and do not let yourselves be burdened again by a yoke of slavery. (Galatians 5:1)

Paul regards adding anything to Jesus, whether circumcision, Mosaic law, good works, or pagan practices, as "slavery." As he told us in a previous reading (4:8–20), we are children of the promise (Sarah), not children of the flesh (Hagar).

Paul continues with what looks like a curious statement: "Mark my words! I, Paul, tell you that if you let yourself be circumcised,

Christ will be of no value to you at all" (5:2). Why the inclusion of "I, Paul"? Remember: Paul didn't write his letters; he dictated them. So, as we imagine him walking around a small room, with Tertius (see Romans 16:22) or some other scribe dutifully recording his inspired utterances, it seems as if Paul suddenly grabs the writing utensil and for emphasis scrawls his own name on the papyrus. It's his way of saying, "I mean business now!"

Paul then spells out the futility of "Jesus plus circumcision" for these Gentile believers in 5:3: "Again, I declare to every man who lets himself be circumcised that he is obligated to obey the whole law." If you decide that your salvation comes from obedience to Moses, you better be prepared to follow all 613 laws and follow them perfectly. Any legal misstep and you're toast! Paul then suggests that the attempt to "be justified"—a way of saying, to be "made right with God"—through this legal obedience indicates that "you have fallen away from grace" (5:4). You might be thinking, *Wait! I've always heard that you* can't *fall away!* While Paul does not define "falling away" with any precision here, it seems that he believes that people can, in fact, abandon the very faith they once held. That's the thrust of the entire Galatian correspondence, after all.

He instead summarizes faith's essence: "The only thing that counts is faith expressing itself through love" (5:6). Look at all that doesn't count in eternal terms: Moses' law. Church ritual. Pagan practices. Anything man-made that we add to the gospel of grace is ultimately in vain.

Paul's next move involves a double entendre. "You were running a good race. Who cut in on you to keep you from obeying the truth?" Notice the language? "Cut in." In the same way that circumcision involves a knife and cutting (and in those days, no anesthesia!), the Galatians have allowed the Judaizing teachers to "cut in" on their once-pure faith. As this letter was read aloud in those congregations,

I am sure that the adolescent boys did their best to stifle their snickers.

For the rest of this paragraph (5:7–12), Paul turns his ire on the false teachers. Not only have they "cut in," but their persuasion doesn't come from Jesus (5:8). It represents unhealthy leaven in otherwise healthy dough (5:9), and they will ultimately pay a heavy price for their deception (5:10). Paul reminds them that the persecution that he suffers is precisely because he refuses to preach "circumcision." This refusal is why he has been thrown out of synagogues throughout the Mediterranean world and why Jewish leaders have insisted that Romans arrest him. In spite of it all, Paul continues to assert his ultimate theological touché:

> In that case the offense of the cross has been abolished. (5:11b)

If you add anything to the cross, you nullify the entire thing. If "everyone" is saved anyway, then the cross was a vicious trick that the Father pulled on the Son. From the Galatian perspective, if another kind of sacrifice was necessary for salvation, the principle applies, and Jesus wasn't the victor on the cross; he was the victim of it. Now we know why Paul tells the Corinthians, "But we preach Christ crucified" (1 Corinthians 1:23).

After that theological apex, Paul then allows his anger to come through. Ready to be shocked and even offended? Referring to the Judaizing teachers, he says, "As for those agitators, I wish they would go the whole way and emasculate themselves" (5:12). If we thought he meant business in 5:2, that's nothing compared to this. His vitriol shows the severity of false teaching and the tenacity with which Paul wants to defend true faith. The embedded shock of his imagery is also a concept with some precedent in the Galatian region, as pagan priests of the goddess Cybele would worship her by castrating themselves.

"Polite society" most likely finds these words and that practice offensive. Yet it shows that Paul is skillful in taking something all too real in the collective mind of the Galatian churches and using it as a warning against any accommodation to false teaching.

Theological conviction. Personal anger. Can they coexist in the same person? What are we to make of a man who could wish this on his opponents, even in jest? I have landed here: when you realize the stakes of his subject, you understand the strength of his language. Paul deals with the salvation of eternal souls, and therefore anyone spoiling the purity of that teaching needs to be resisted and rebuked. Perhaps we're offended by his language because we've tolerated a few too many modern versions of false teachers in our own churches.

When it comes to the things of God, the higher the stakes, the stronger the language.

DAY ELEVEN
Galatians 5:13-26

....

We come today to the best-known and most quoted section of the Galatian letter. However, like many "best known" and "most quoted" parts of Scripture, its popularity is due in some measure to taking things out of context. So, let's put them in context.

Paul has just finished a section in which he uses some shocking language (see 5:12) to reiterate his primary theme: "It is for freedom that Christ has set us free" (5:1). Christ didn't come to set us back into a performance mindset but instead to give us a relational/positional spirit-set. Once we're saved by grace through faith, we don't have to backtrack to live by works all over again.

Yet the freedom that the gospel provides and Paul proclaims presents us with a dilemma: How do you not use that freedom as a license to sin? As long as salvation is by grace, why not "sin it up" so that God has to pour out even more grace? This is the question Paul refers to in Galatians 5:13, as he advises, "[d]o not use your freedom to indulge the flesh." Paul dealt with this matter earlier, in his letter to the Roman church (Romans 6–8) and he turns to it again now. His answer divides neatly into three paragraphs (5:16–18; 5:19–21; 5:22–26). These paragraphs fall into two literary structures: particularization and contrast.

In particularization, an author announces his main point and then spends time spelling out the implications of that point in particulars. It's the opposite of generalization, where an author will "collect the dots" of specific examples and later "connect the dots" with a general summary.

So, in Galatians 5:16, Paul gives his general truth:

So I say, walk by the Spirit, and you will not gratify the desires of the flesh.

The key to not using grace as license is sin isn't trying harder. It's trusting more. It's surrendering moment by moment to the Spirit, who lives in you and through you. As I often say while preaching, surrender your impulses so you don't surrender to them. Then 5:17–19 spells out the particulars of what living by the Spirit involves:

Be alert to the ways your sinful nature is in conflict with the Spirit.

The result is you do not do what you want . . . which means that in Christ you really want to do good!

Allow yourself to be led by the Spirit.

The following two paragraphs (5:19–21 and 5:22–26) are examples of how Paul uses contrast to make his point. He teaches us what life in the Spirit is by first showing us what it is not:

sexual immorality, impurity, and debauchery
idolatry and witchcraft
hatred
discord
jealousy
fits of rage
selfish ambition
dissensions
factions and envy
drunkenness
orgies

Notice that although the list springs from a vertical deficit (not being led by the Spirit), it manifests in horizontal relationships (almost all the sins deal with how we treat one another).

The verdict on this kind of life and lack of faith? "Those who live like this will not inherit the kingdom of God" (v. 21).

After that Debbie Downer of a paragraph, Paul puts a much more positive spin on what comes next.

"But" is how 5:22 begins, letting you know the power of the impending contrast.

But the fruit of the Spirit is . . .

Note that it's not "fruits" of the Spirit, but "fruit," singular. That's why we read "The fruit of the Spirit *is*" and not "The fruits of the Spirits *are*." They're not ours to pick and choose; they're not even the object of our faith pursuit. Instead, the object of our faith is Spirit-filling, and this particular array of "fruit" is the result. What life emerges when the Holy Spirit has all of you? It's a list I've memorized if only occasionally demonstrated.

love
joy
peace
forbearance (patience)
kindness
goodness
faithfulness
gentleness
self-control

Isn't it interesting that self-control is a fruit of the Spirit and self-expression (what we call self-actualization in our current culture) is not?

Paul closes this section by reminding us that this kind of life is possible. Think of all the relational conflict it can prevent! When we keep in step with the Spirit, it usually puts us *out* of step with the self-driven impulses of the world.

How much of you does the Holy Spirit have?

DAY TWELVE
Galatians 6:1-10

I f yesterday's reading was an example of *particularization* in which Paul gives the general principle first and then particularizes it through the passage, today's reading demonstrates the opposite: *generalization*. In this section, Paul will give us nine verses full of very detailed commands and then will summarize it all with the general statement of Galatians 6:10:

> Therefore, as we have opportunity, let us do good to all people, especially to those who belong to the family of believers.

This passage, then, doesn't lead with the "point" but builds to it.

What are the particulars that lead to the summary statement of Galatians 6:10? They are many. In fact, for a letter that is so heavy on "grace" and so against "law," these words sound almost legalistic! Perhaps a kinder, gentler, and more accurate word to use would be "practical." Listen to Paul's following counsel:

> Restore one who is caught in sin. (6:1, paraphrased)

Don't enable, but don't ostracize. What a balance! Guess what? Those who "restore" a friend will one day be the friend in need of restoration.

> Watch yourself so you're not tempted. (6:1, paraphrased)

What kinds of channels do you allow in your home, and what kind of websites do you visit? What protections are in place? Couples, do you have each other's smartphone passwords? As much as I can as a pastor, I don't merely recommend that practice to couples under my counsel, but I insist on it. What hope does any troubled couple have if they can't be honest with that most basic of information?

> Carry each other's burdens. (6:2)

In 2021, I delivered a sermon that addressed this point: "Influencers don't wait to be asked because they see what others don't and do what others won't." People of influence and impact, then, don't ask, "What can I do?" Nor do they say, "Call me if you need anything." They think proactively rather than reactively. That mindset is what Paul drives at here.

> If you think you're something you deceive yourself. (6:3, paraphrased)

You're not all that until you're all his. Galatians 6:3 is not found on any church sign boards, Christian bumper stickers, or even many tattoos of faith. But it should be on all of them.

> Each one should test their own actions. Then they can take pride in themselves alone, without comparing themselves to someone else. (6:4)

Of all phrases in this section to memorize, "without comparing themselves to somebody else" should top our list!

> Carry your own load. (6:5)

> Share good things with those who instruct you. (6:6, paraphrased)

> You will reap what you sow. (6:7–9, paraphrased)

Ponder those final verses. These words (echoed in 2 Corinthians 9:6–15) are as close as biblical faith comes to karma. Karma has a grain of truth in it: you do in fact reap much of what you sow. Yet, like fate, karma is ironclad and irresistible. Our Hindu and Buddhist friends believe it is inescapable. We who believe in grace believe differently. In grace, we're not graded on a curve; we're graded on the cross.

Karma imprisons, but grace frees.

DAY THIRTEEN
Galatians 6:11–18

Paul's letter to the Galatian churches opened with a mixture of vitriol and candor. How will he close it? When you've openly called those reading your letter "foolish," how do you make amends by letter's end? Do you need to? Or want to? Those are some of the questions we'll address in today's reading.

As Paul concludes his letter, he does so by giving us yet another reminder of the dictation process: "See what large letters I use as I write to you with my own hand!" (6:11). This likely means that in an effort to make his conclusion more personal, Paul grabs the writing utensil from his scribe and pens the final paragraph himself. The "large letters" suggest that because of the eye condition to which he refers in Galatians 4:12–15, he has to use the kind of sprawling handwriting that fits a man who can barely see. We might say, "now I'm moving from font size 12 to 24!"

After that note of personality and vulnerability, Paul returns to the main point of his epistle: "Those who want to impress people by means of the flesh are trying to compel you to be circumcised. The only reason they do this is to avoid being persecuted for the cross of Christ" (6:12). This is a new twist to the book-long saga. Judaizers "Judaize" so they themselves will not be persecuted by synagogue leadership! They don't keep the full law themselves. Who can? But they insist that the Gentile converts to Jesus from Galatia follow Moses first.

Now listen to one of the most glorious of all sentences that Paul ever writes:

> May I never boast except in the cross of our Lord Jesus Christ, through which the world has been crucified to me, and I to the world. (6:14)

Unlike the other apostles, Paul did not witness Jesus' persecution in real time. Yet its impact and importance are never far from his mind. The cross is the source of his identity and his joy. What matters to Paul is not the status of a man's circumcision or lack thereof; "what counts is the new creation" (6:15). He has already said as much to the Corinthians: "Therefore, if anyone is in Christ, the new creation has come: the old has gone, the new is here!" (2 Corinthians 5:17).

Paul gives passing reference to the wounds he has suffered for his faith in Galatians 6:17. He speaks here of being "branded" in Jesus by the marks of his suffering for his Messiah and Lord. His passion for the rescue of the Galatian Christians is so intense that his own pain is merely an afterthought.

He closes his letter on a conciliatory note and with a transformational word: "grace." Not *works*. Not *law*. Not *achievement*. Not *performance*. And certainly not *circumcision*. *Grace*. May the grace that has saved you be the grace that shapes you.

What Paul says to the Galatians, I say to you. The grace that has saved you and now shapes you is never average but always amazing. *Grace* is also a word that might just appear in the next letter we'll explore together, Paul's letter to the Ephesians.

There is no such hymn as "Average Grace," is there? Grace always amazes.

Introduction
To Ephesians

Ephesians brought me back from the brink.

As a twenty-five-year-old young adult, having been a Christian for eight years, I was on a downward trajectory. Hollow in my attitudes, cynical in my relationships, and trending toward an abandonment of the very faith that had given me my identity and assurance.

While on that particular precipice, I wandered into a church I had never attended and had a conversation with a pastor I had never met. His direction?

"Read Ephesians."

"Read Ephesians," he repeated, "and know that when Paul speaks of a 'Spirit of wisdom and revelation' (1:17), he's not speaking of a relic of ancient times. The Spirit of wisdom and revelation still moves, still inhabits, and longs to fill you up with all the fullness of God."

Not knowing any better, I followed instructions.

That pastor was as good as his word, and Ephesians was, in fact, better than promised. I was brought back from the brink swiftly enough and comprehensively enough that scarcely a year later I was in seminary and preparing for pastoral ministry. My living relationship with Jesus Christ has never been the same, and Paul's inspired words in Ephesians were the catalyst.

Perhaps you're on the brink. Hollow in your attitudes, cynical in your relationships, and in danger of abandoning the same faith that has given you identity and assurance. Maybe you're thinking the Bible doesn't really make much sense or, even if it does, it's no longer really relevant to the complexities of life in the 2020s.

If so, I can tell you from personal experience that you have come to the right place. My prayer is that this guide will help the words of Ephesians come alive for you in the same way they did—and still do—for me.

May God grant you a spirit of wisdom and revelation so that you will love the Scriptures so you can adore the Savior.

DAY FOURTEEN
Ephesians 1:1–14

....

I have been reading the New Testament for a long time, but I realize that I am only now learning how to read its epistles. To read the New Testament well, you need to read the epistles carefully.

Here's what I've recently discovered. For years, I have read these documents as if they were examples of **modern American letter writing**. But as noted earlier, that's not what they are.

They are instead examples of **ancient Greek speechmaking**. And there is a world of difference between those two genres.

The opening chapter of Ephesians is one of the best texts to explore. As you read, keep in mind that Paul was himself Jewish, while Ephesus is in modern-day Turkey. Those who received his letter were Gentiles. Pay attention to the pronouns, as they make all the difference.

> Paul, an apostle of Christ Jesus by the will of God, to God's holy people in Ephesus, the faithful in Christ Jesus:
>
> Grace and peace to **you** from God our Father and the Lord Jesus Christ.
>
> Praise be to the God and Father of our Lord Jesus Christ, who has blessed us in the heavenly realms with every spiritual blessing in Christ. For he chose **us** in him before the creation of the world to be holy and blameless in his sight. In love he predestined **us** for adoption to sonship through Jesus Christ, in accordance with his pleasure and will— to the praise of his glorious grace, which he has freely given **us** in the One he loves. In him **we** have redemption through his blood, the forgiveness of sins, in accordance with the riches of God's grace that he lavished on **us**. With all wisdom and understanding, he made known to **us** the mystery of his will according to his good pleasure, which he purposed in Christ, to be put into effect when the times reach their fulfillment—to bring unity to all things in heaven and on earth under Christ.

In him **we** were also chosen, having been predestined according to the plan of him who works out everything in conformity with the purpose of his will, in order that **we**, who were the first to put our hope in Christ, might be for the praise of his glory. (Ephesians 1:1–12)

If you read this according to the rules of modern American letter writing, all the "us" and "we" references are a way of including you, the reader, in what the author is saying. So those of us who are modern American Christians assume from the beginning that Paul is including the original Ephesians as well as the current readers with these opening words.

Except that's not what he is doing. Ephesians is not an example of modern American letter writing. Instead—again—it is ancient Greek speechmaking.

In the argument that Paul is building for Ephesians, "we" and "us" refer to Paul and his kin, the Jews. You get the gist of what he is doing if you imagine that he is standing on a platform with two fellow Jews, addressing a room full of Gentiles. With each "we" and "us," he points to his Hebrew colleagues on the stage.

Verse 12 is especially critical to this understanding: "we, who were the first to put our hope in Christ . . ." Who were the first to hope in Christ? Not the Ephesians! Instead, Romans 1:16 tells us who were the first to hope in Christ: the apostles, including Paul: "For I am not ashamed of the Gospel, because it is the power of God that brings salvation to everyone who believes: *first to the Jew, then to the Gentile.*"

Lights just went on in brains all across the fruited plain! Or at least the one that's in your head.

Understanding that "we" are the Jews and not the broader, fledgling Christian community goes a long way in explaining all the references to predestination and to being "chosen." That's how we understand God's relationship with Israel.

After that lengthy opening section, with all its focus on "we" and "us," everything changes in verse 13:

> And **you** also were included in Christ when **you** heard the message of truth, the gospel of your salvation. When **you** believed, you were marked in him with a seal, the promised Holy Spirit, who is a deposit guaranteeing our inheritance until the redemption of those who are God's possession—to the praise of his glory. (vv. 13–14)

Here the transition from "we" to "you" is instantaneous, dramatic, and purposeful.

Imagine that Paul suddenly points to his audience and says, "And you Gentiles were included in Christ just as we were." This introduction is a compelling example of ancient Greek speechmaking.

From the beginning, then, Ephesians is about this divine fusion of "we" and "you"; the creation of something brand-new out of "us" and "them."

When you understand how the Bible was written and compiled, what it says is even more powerful and compelling.

DAY FIFTEEN
Ephesians 1:15-23

Ephesians began with a master class in pronouns. The "us," "we," and "our" make all the difference, as does the awareness that we are listening to an ancient Greek speech rather reading a modern American letter.

As we pick up Paul's letter to the Ephesians, the pronouns portion of the spoken word performance has just taken a dramatic shift beginning at verse 13, as you saw yesterday:

> And **you also** were included in Christ when **you** heard the message of truth, the gospel of **your** salvation. When **you** believed, **you** were marked in him with a seal, the promised Holy Spirit, who is a deposit guaranteeing our inheritance until the redemption of those who are God's possession—to the praise of his glory. (Ephesians 1:13–14)

For the rest of this section, the "yous" have it. Not the "youse" from Long Island, but the "you" from Ephesus, Gentile believers who are in fact the second to believe in Christ. This has been Paul's thrust from the letter to the Romans onward: "first to the Jew, then to the Gentile" (Romans 1:16).

Notice how the pronouns dominate today's reading:

1:15: *your* faith
1:15: *your* love
1:16: giving thanks for *you*
1:16: remembering *you* in my prayers
1:17: give *you* the Spirit of wisdom and revelation
1:17: so that *you* may know him better
1:18: the eyes of *your* heart
1:18: the hope to which he has called *you*

Paul is addressing his Gentile friends from Ephesus in a direct yet loving way. All that is prelude to verse 1:19: "and his incomparably great power to **us** who believe." We're all in this together! Jew and Gentile alike are in the same power-receiving mode. When you know what Paul is doing and how he is doing it, it's more remarkable, not less. Such awareness makes the Bible feel more inspired, not less. The message feels more exalted, precisely because it is birthed within the nitty-gritty of life, church conflict, and redemption. I've said this before but it is worth another mention: no New Testament correspondence emerges out of thin air. Each letter is written to a real church going through real issues involving real people in real time. In Ephesus, that issue was "How do we form one body out of two distinct people?" Paul's answer will come as a thunderbolt in chapter 2 of Ephesians.

Jesus continues to make his incomparable power available to us who believe even in this present age. Are you receptive to his power in your life?

DAY SIXTEEN
Ephesians 2:1-10

....

As we have opened Ephesians up in this study, we have learned that it is not a case of *modern American letter writing* but instead of *ancient Greek speechmaking.* With that realization comes the understanding that the pronouns Paul uses make all the difference in the meaning of his letter. "You" Ephesian Gentiles are being melded with "we" Jewish Christians into one glorious grace-filled, blood-bought body of Christ. The church, then, is the real-time expression of Ephesians 1:10: how God brings "unity to all things in heaven and on earth under Christ." Whatever else Ephesians is about, it is fundamentally about unity, not for its own sake but to bring glory to our Messiah.

It's vital to reinforce that background, because today's section (2:1–10) is the most well-known parcel in the book, featuring the most-memorized verses of the letter, Ephesians 2:8–9:

> For it is by grace you have been saved, through faith—and this is not from yourselves, it is the gift of God—not by works so that no one can boast.

I've memorized this verse. Maybe you have as well. Even when I haven't known it word for word, I've known where it is, what it says, and have used it mostly as a weapon against those who say that heaven is a reward for good living. If Ephesians as a book is primarily about getting your sorry soul into heaven after you die, then that's the summary of what Ephesians 2:8–9 means. However, we've already seen and experienced together that Ephesians is about much more than that. These two verses have a richer and deeper meaning when we read them in *context.* Context is everything.

For today's context, look at verse 1: "As for you, you were dead in your transgressions and sin." Who is the "you"? These are the Ephesian Gentiles who before they heard about Christ were involved in idol worship and pagan religion. The result of that? Spiritually speaking, they were the walking dead!

Paul continues his riff about the "deadness" of the Ephesians before they met Jesus, commenting on the way "in which [they] used to live when [they] followed the ways of this world and of the ruler of the kingdom of the air" (2:2). Again, think of those objectionable and even repulsive pagan practices, like praying to statues, consorting with temple prostitutes, and sacrificing children to appease angry gods. At this stage, some of the Ephesians may have been hanging their heads in shame as they remembered how they used to worship and live.

But then Paul inserts a stunner: "All of us also . . ." *Who* also? "Us Jews!" Paul is saying, "We too lived apart from God and for ourselves!" At this, the Gentiles must have looked up in surprise and said, "Wait! I thought as the chosen people you all were special and holy." Paul rushes to assure them: "Like the rest, we were by nature deserving of wrath" (2:3). Who are "the rest"? Gentiles! Who is "we"? Jews, again! This is breakthrough thinking. Being born Jewish didn't magically make one born righteous. Not at all. Instead, what Jew and Gentile alike shared in common is that they were both objects of wrath by nature. All humankind, then, is naughty by nature! What a predicament!

The discomfort we feel at this stage is precisely where Paul wants us. Why?

His next words explain: "But . . . God . . ." (2:4). Hallelujah! Rooted in the grace, mercy, and redemptive love on our behalf, God "made us alive with Christ even when we were dead in transgressions" (2:5). Who is the "us"? Jew and Gentile alike. We share an inborn alienation from God at birth, and then a reborn resurrection in Christ. There's not one standard for Jew and another for Gentile. All alike sit under condemnation, and then all alike rise in grace. God is good, extraordinarily good.

From there, praise and adoration roll off Paul's tongue in 2:6–9. We already have the "best seat in the house," as my friend Carolyn Moore calls it (2:6), all so that God may to his great delight and to our great blessing "show the incomparable riches of his grace, expressed in his kindness to us [all of us, regardless of ethnicity] in Christ Jesus" (2:7). With all that buildup, Paul reiterates the truth with which we began in 2:8–9, verses we now know don't stand alone as a private path to heaven but instead stand among a breathtaking explanation of the goodness of God.

By grace we are saved. These words reveal our heavenly path. In their original setting, however, they're not about my sin-sick soul escaping its well-deserved punishment. They're about our great God, who is building a grace-filled and blood-bought church of people who otherwise would share nothing in common.

The result of all this? Ephesians 2:10 says it: "For we are God's handiwork, created in Christ Jesus to do good works, which God prepared in advance for us to do." We're not saved by doing good, but we are saved for doing good. Some of the best "good" we can do is to live as an unlikely community (the church) who has been chased, caught, and kept by an incomparable God.

Isolated Scripture verses don't stand alone as a private path to heaven but instead stand among as a breathtaking explanation of the goodness of God.

DAY SEVENTEEN
Ephesians 2:11–22

....

Think of all the things you do automatically, those mundane activities that you have done with such repetition you no longer have to think about how to do them: brush your teeth, take a step, turn on your car's ignition. These and many others are automatic because your muscles have memorized how to do them. It's why once you learn how to ride a bicycle, you can't unlearn that skill, barring a catastrophic accident or injury. Muscle memory is the reason for it all. The same is true with your daily scripture readings. You're building muscle memory of the spiritual kind. The words of scripture are implanting themselves deeply in your brain and in your psyche. It's becoming automatic that you're learning to think biblically. What a privilege to help guide you on this sacred journey. With that, pause and ask God to grow your muscle memory as you read Paul's meditation for today.

If you had asked me a few years ago for the central thrust of Ephesians, I would have taken you right to 2:8–9:

> For it is by grace you have been saved, through faith—and this is not from yourselves, it is the gift of God—not by works, so that no one can boast.

If it was good enough to inspire Martin Luther to start the Reformation, it's good enough to serve as the main point of the book, right? Ephesians is a mini-manifesto about salvation by grace. Well, Ephesians includes teaching about *sola fide*, but that's not its heart.

Another possible answer to the Ephesians question might have come from the glorious prayers in 1:17–23 and 3:16–21, prayers that served no small role in my own call to ministry. Based on those prayers—and praying them in isolation from the rest of the book—

Ephesians is about tapping into the incredible power that resides simultaneously at the center of the universe and in the middle of our hearts! If that doesn't get your spiritual adrenaline flowing, nothing will.

That's part of Ephesians' contribution, but it's still not the primary purpose behind Paul's letter to the burgeoning Christian community there. To discover Paul's core message, remember how the letter begins in 1:1–14: a divine fusion of "we" and "you," a melding of Jew and Gentile, a creation of one new community out of what had been discord and division. We see the culmination of that theme in 2:11–22, a section again dominated by the pronouns:

> Therefore, remember that formerly **you** who are Gentiles by birth and called "uncircumcised" by those who call themselves "the circumcision" (which is done in the body by human hands)—remember that at that time **you** were separate from Christ, excluded from citizenship in Israel and foreigners to the covenants of the promise, without hope and without God in the world. But now in Christ Jesus **you** who once were far away have been brought near by the blood of Christ.
>
> For he himself is **our** peace, who has made the two groups one and has destroyed the barrier, the dividing wall of hostility, by setting aside in his flesh the law with its commands and regulations. His purpose was to create in himself one new humanity out of the two, thus making peace, and in one body to reconcile both of them to God through the cross, by which he put to death their hostility. He came and preached peace to **you who were far away** and peace to **those who were near**. For through him we both have access to the Father by one Spirit.
>
> Consequently, **you** are no longer foreigners and strangers, but fellow citizens with God's people and also members of his household, built on the foundation of the apostles and prophets, with Christ Jesus himself as the chief cornerstone. In him the whole building is joined together and rises to become a holy temple in the Lord. And in him **you** too are being built together to become a dwelling in which God lives by his Spirit.

The entire section is brilliant, but it's 2:15 that contains the nutshell: "to create in himself one new humanity out of the two." Paul wrote Ephesians to let Jew and Gentile alike know that when they reside together in a person called Christ, God creates an entirely new race of people.

People no longer connected by tribe. People bought by blood.

People no longer distinguished by race. People identified by resurrection.

People no longer separated by class. People united by cross.

The "you" and the "we" become gloriously swept up in the "him." Hallelujah!

Such unity within diversity is not simply for its own sake. It doesn't stem from a politically correct mindset of "can't we all just get along?" This kind of diversity happens only as the gift of God and is lived out for the glory of Christ by the power of the Holy Spirit.

In your local church and mine, diversity is never the cause. It's always the result. When Jesus remains the cause, he ends up bringing his friends with him.

DAY EIGHTEEN
Ephesians 3:1-13

....

As if we needed further proof of the role of the pronouns in determining the heart of Ephesians, 3:1 removes all doubt:

> For this reason I, Paul, [am] the prisoner of Christ for the sake of **you Gentiles**.

There it is, in plain English; that is, plain Greek in the original writing and dictating. As he writes Ephesians, Paul is under house arrest in Rome for the crime of being a Christian. As with Jesus before him, his accusers were both the Jews, who took offense that he claimed Jesus as Messiah and that he took the gospel to non-Jews, and the Romans, who had the power to carry out his execution. So, when Paul says his imprisonment was for the "sake of you Gentiles," he is not exaggerating. He could have adapted his message to avoid trouble, but he chose not to. Instead of watering the gospel down, he heated it up. He knew the most profound of truths: when the church modifies the Word to satisfy the world, it doesn't win more converts; it only earns more contempt. Paul preached the whole gospel to the whole world and paid the whole price.

From there, Paul goes on in Ephesians 3:2–7 to reinforce much of what he has been saying from the opening words of the book.

> Grace . . . was given to me for you. (3:2)

> The mystery I teach and preach was revealed to me and to the other apostles and prophets. (3:5, paraphrased)

We did not figure the gospel out. We didn't discover it. We didn't conjure it up. The gospel has been the plan from the beginning of time, and only now (meaning Paul's "now") has God graciously revealed it to us. We couldn't figure it out, so God sent it down. Without revelation there is no salvation.

Paul spells out the mystery in verse 6: "This mystery is that through the gospel the Gentiles are heirs together with Israel, members together of one body, and sharers together in the promise in Christ Jesus."

Do you see the repetition? Note the neon light? *Together, together, together.* Gentiles and Jews are heirs together. Gentiles and Jews comprise the body of Christ together. Gentiles and Jews share the promise of Jesus together. There is no "Path A for Jews" and "Path B for Gentiles." No Jewish heaven and Gentile heaven. All experience God's grace together.

If you're of a certain age or listen to certain vintage radio stations, you may be going all Youngbloods right now:

Everybody get together
Try to love one another right now.
(The Youngbloods, "Get Together," by Chet Powers, in *The Youngbloods*, RCA Victor, 1966, vinyl.)

The song is nostalgic for some and a revelation for others. Yet there is also a critical difference between it and Ephesians. Notice the imperative in the chorus: "Try to love one another right now." Ephesians 3 is in the indicative. Everything Paul promises has been accomplished in Christ. We don't do more. We live into what Jesus has already done. What a difference! What a gospel! You can live into this "together" gospel not as you try to "be better" but instead as you access the power Jesus has already poured out to you to become perfectly mature in your discipleship, even as your Father in heaven is perfect.

In Ephesians 3:8–10, Paul marvels that he, "the least of all the Lord's people," should be given the privilege of communicating the mystery that was revealed to him. God first revealed the mystery of Gentile inclusion to him and did so in order that Paul would then transmit that mystery to the world. Paul can barely wrap his head around the ways God has given him gifts and graces for such work. That's why he puts these thrilling words in Ephesians 3:8b:

> This grace was given me: to preach to the Gentiles the boundless riches of Christ.

All that is why Paul concludes his thought in 3:12 with "In him we may approach God with freedom and confidence." That wording is similar to Hebrews 4:16: "Let us . . . approach God's throne of grace with confidence." It's not a "throne of merit." It's not a "throne of achievement." It's a "throne of grace." We can cast timidity aside and approach it with confidence because our intimacy in prayer is not earned by our performance. It's given by Jesus' sacrifice.

Since it's not a "throne of merit," but a "throne of grace," I invite you to write your prayer to God in the space below.

DAY NINETEEN
Ephesians 3:14-21

In today's slice of Ephesians, we come to the second prayer that Paul inserts into his letter, the first having come in 1:15–23. Taken together, the two prayers show how Paul simply gets carried away with the love and might of Jesus while he is dictating his letter. In modern speak, the prayers are a combination of rabbit trails and streams of consciousness—except they're inspired, eternal, true, and downright perfect.

Look closely at this one. It starts with "For this reason" (3:14). What reason? What has Paul just said in 3:7–13? The mystery of the gospel's availability to Jew and Gentile alike was revealed to him, both to receive it and then to transmit it. He both inherits and heralds grace! For that reason, Paul says in 3:12 that we can "approach God with freedom and confidence." Now, in 3:14–21, he's going to show us what such a prayer looks like.

Paul states, "I kneel before the Father" (3:14). The language there is actually stronger than "kneel." It's more like, "I fall prostrate before him" or "I fall on my face." Posture influences prayer, and I invite you to experiment. I have been sitting and writing the majority of my prayers over the last couple of years. Perhaps it's time to spend some time kneeling and some time on my face before the Lord.

Paul affirms the Fatherhood of God over the names and the nations in verse 15, and then in verse 16 his prayer gets down to business. This is also where this portion of the letter begins to sound quite similar to 1:15–23. Here are verses 16–17 of Ephesians 3:

> I pray that out of his glorious riches he may strengthen you with power through his Spirit in your inner being so that Christ may dwell in your hearts through faith.

Interestingly, that passage is one of the relatively few times that Paul speaks of Christ "in your hearts"; he is much more likely to urge his readers to live their lives "in Christ." Most of us love the idea of inviting Jesus into our hearts—and that's good; that's true; that's right—but I wonder if we miss something of the vastness of faith by rarely speaking of living our lives in the enormity of Jesus. Rather than compress him into our hearts, perhaps we ought to expand our lives into his Spirit.

Paul elaborates further in 3:17b-18:

> And I pray that you, being rooted and established in love, may have power, together with all the Lord's holy people, to grasp how wide and long and high and deep is the love of Christ, and to know this love that surpasses knowledge.

This phrase is loaded up with meaning and packed with beauty. Look at the connection. We need power to grasp. We need divine strength simply to understand. That's not a combination you often see together. Usually, you need power to do and God's help to accomplish. This is different. God's love for us is so incomprehensible that we need divine power to wrap our minds around it. Our minds are feeble and need shoring up even to begin the journey of understanding God's love for us. We do this "together with all the Lord's holy people" (3:18). You and I cannot figure this out alone. We can't comprehend the infinity and the intimacy of God's love without the community of Christ surrounding us. I call it a "living relationship with Jesus Christ," because living things don't live alone. They grow, stretch, and strengthen in relationship, in community.

I saw this example in a young adult life group that I led within my church. Conversation was lively, prayer was genuine, and then at the end, I got into my car to drive home, while they hung around in the parking lot to continue the kind of human interaction that leads to life. It was glorious to see, especially after a nearly eighteen-month hiatus due to the 2020 Covid Pandemic where such meetings were rare and fraught with anxiety. This time there was no anxiety; it was beautiful. All had begun to comprehend the incomprehensible. Each of us there was loved, chased, caught, and kept by Jesus "the pursuer."

The result of all this for Paul? "That you may be filled to the measure of all the fullness of God" (3:19). Compare that with the closing of the first prayer in 1:23: "which is his body, the fullness of him who fills everything in every way."

Each day, then, you begin as an empty vessel into which God wants to pour all fullness. God is never finished with the job of growing you or stretching you. God will discomfort you so that God can enlighten you. Offer yourself to God for that purpose today, expecting the kind of blessings that come from Paul's "doxology," in 3:20–21:

> Now to him who is able to do immeasurably more than all we ask or imagine, according to his power that is at work within us, to him be glory in the church and in Christ Jesus throughout all generations forever and ever! Amen.

We can only comprehend the infinity and the intimacy of God's love from within the community of Christ that surrounds us.

DAY TWENTY
Ephesians 4:1-16

··

Ephesians makes a major pivot as chapter 4 begins. Paul has spent three chapters (remember that the chapter and verse numbers were added hundreds of years later by the church) establishing the theological foundations of unity between Jew and Gentile believers in Ephesus. Now he turns in rather dramatic fashion to tell them the practical implications of living out that unity. Paul has used this pattern before, as Romans 1–11 laid out a similar though expanded theological framework around "first for the Jew, then for the Gentile" and Romans 12–16 laid out with great specificity how that church needs to embody the truth that has given it birth.

We see the transition here in Ephesians through a shift in verb tenses. Up until now, it has mostly been in the *indicative*: the emphasis on what Christ has done and the unity he has provided. In 4:1-3, Paul shifts to the *imperative:* here's what you're to do. And what are they to do? What are Paul's imperative verbs?

> I urge.
> Live a worthy life.
> Be completely humble.
> Be patient.
> Bear with one another in love.
> Keep the unity of the Spirit through the bond of peace.

Read over that list a couple of times. Now read it out loud. Those are the kind of words that belong in the permanent background of our minds, our human operating system, so that they work their way into our subconscious and shape how we respond and live.

After those imperatives, Paul shifts back to indicative mode as he substantiates the reason for the church's unity. Look now at verses 4–6:

There is one body and one Spirit, just as you were called to one hope when you were called; one Lord, one faith, one baptism; one God and Father of all, who is over all and through all and in all.

One body—one Spirit—one hope—one Lord—one faith—one baptism—one God. Our "one God" has revealed one Self to us in three persons: Father, Son, and Holy Spirit.

In verses 7–10, Paul uses Psalm 68 to demonstrate that in Christ our God has ascended into the heavens not to escape the world but instead to "fill the whole universe" (4:10) with God's presence. There's that word "fullness" again! From that position in glory, God gives every good gift that every person has ever enjoyed. This is an echo of James 1:17: "Every good and perfect gift is from above, coming down from the Father of the heavenly lights, who does not change like shifting shadows."

Some of the gifts that God pours out involve specific roles for church leadership. As you read about these differing gifts, know that they're not for "platform people" or "ordained people" or even for "celebrity preachers." They are for the church, which might well mean you.

Apostles
Prophets
Evangelists
Pastors
Teachers

This is not a comprehensive list—Romans 12 and 1 Corinthians 12 do a more precise job of that—but it's an important one. In many church circles this list is called the "fivefold ministry." And what is the purpose of fivefold ministry? Ephesians 4:12 tells us it is "to equip his people for works of service, so that the body of Christ may be built up."

The job, then, of any pastor, teacher, or leader in the church is not so much to do the ministry as to multiply ministry by preparing and encouraging the people of the church to embrace the work for themselves. The most consistently clear examples of this in our setting are the hundreds of equipped volunteers who mentor our children, welcome worshipers, and lead our groups and classes. In those cases, staff knows that a major part of their job is to find and prepare people like you to be the church and carry out its mission. If you don't have a church you call home, I invite you to look for one whose goal is more about "sending out" than "filling up," a church that measures its effectiveness not by the number of people who come into worship but by the number who go out to serve. One day that will include you.

What's the result of equipped people engaging in works of service? Paul says, "so that the body of Christ may be built up until we all reach unity in the faith and in the knowledge of the Son of God and become mature, attaining to the whole measure of the fullness of Christ" (4:12–13).

Preparing people for ministry leads to unity, which results in maturity, which reflects divinity. What an assignment but what a privilege!

That tells me that disunity is never a church's primary problem. Immaturity is. A fighting church—and we've all been part of one—is at its heart an immature church.

Perhaps that's why Paul concludes this section in 4:14–16 with a promise of the fruit of maturity-based unity. We won't be vulnerable to false teaching and doctrinal fads but will instead continue our trajectory of growth. Jesus is both the goal and the source of our maturity (4:15) and provides the structure through which such growth happens: his body (4:16). I love that Paul uses the word "ligament" in 4:16. You may or may not know this, but the word "religion" has its roots in the Latin word for "ligament." "Religion" has a negative connotation today, but I believe it's time to redeem that word when we understand what it really means. We're in this together, joined in the great adhesive of the body of Christ. We will be neither unified nor mature in isolation but only in community.

Have you been joined together by the great adhesive that is the body of Christ?

DAY TWENTY-ONE
Ephesians 4:17-28

P aul's letter to the church in Ephesus made a dramatic turn from the *indicative* to the *imperative*—from "this is true" to "now here's how to live"—at the beginning of what we have as chapter 4. In today's reading, Paul's instructions along those lines go into overdrive.

Look how he begins: "So I tell you this, and insist on it in the Lord, that you must no longer live as the Gentiles do." Do you know what's ironic about that? The Ephesians are Gentiles! To see just how "Gentile" the residents of that city are, check out Acts 19:23–41 which is subtitled "The Riot in Ephesus."

Reading the letter to the Ephesians alongside the historical account of what happened in Ephesus shows again how the Bible is a library. The book of Acts describes the expansion of the church in the years just after Jesus died and rose again. Paul is the central figure of the last half of Acts, and he got into trouble in almost every city he visited. Why? Preaching the gospel! The trouble in Ephesus is the most dramatic of his experiences, as the rise of the Jesus movement led naturally to the demise of the idol making business. When it starts impacting the profit margin, you know that means business! Acts 19 details how the "Idol Makers Guild" started an uprising against Paul and his message. Paul survived—barely—but the entire incident shows the power of idolatry and pagan worship among the Gentile Ephesians. It is also no doubt in the back of Paul's mind as he writes this letter.

Paul begins this exhortation by essentially saying, "Don't act like who you are!" or rather "who you were." In the rest of 4:17–19, he describes why the pagan life centered around idol worship is so empty using words such as these:

futile thinking
darkened understanding
separated from God due to ignorance and hardened hearts
lost sensitivity
given over to indulge every sensuality and impurity
full of greed

Notice that worship starts in the mind, moves to the heart, and leads to behavior. What Paul elaborates on is people who have lost the capacity to feel guilty for their own sin. They instead become hollowed out, relentlessly pursuing the next "high," the next "hit," the next pleasure. As any addict will tell you, no high is ever as good as that first one. The law of diminishing returns is the driving factor in any descent into compulsion and chaos. Paul knew it and had seen it. He is describing this reality in the language of his time.

In 4:20–24, Paul shifts to encouragement: That's who you were but it's not who you are. Notice the "put off" in 4:22 (and 4:25) as well as the "put on" in 4:24. In Paul's mind, the Christian life consists of stripping off the old outfit (idolatry) and completely re-clothing one's self in Jesus. Jesus is not an accessory; he is the entire ensemble. The purpose of our new clothing is in 4:24. We were "created to be like God in true righteousness and holiness." For Paul, holiness looks like this:

Speak truthfully.
Express anger in a way that does not simmer and does not sin.
Do not give the devil a foothold.
Stop stealing.

Stop stealing? It's interesting that he had to mention that. Perhaps theft was a way of life in Ephesus, and getting away with it was a mark of cunning and skill. But note the reason why Paul wants the Ephesians to stop stealing and start working: so that the people in the church "may have something to share with those in need" (4:28).

With that, we'll pause and pick up Paul's string of commands in our next section. Have a great day, living as who you are now and not who you were then.

> ***Is Jesus an accessory to your life or is he the entire ensemble?***

DAY TWENTY-TWO
Ephesians 4:29–5:2

....

Paul offers us a short slice of reading today, though one packed with both meaning and instruction. We learned that Ephesians 4 represents a pivot in the book from the *indicative* to the *imperative;* from *explanation* to *exhortation;* from *"this is true"* to *"now here's how you live."* This short slice today is quite possibly the most "imperative" section of them all. Here's how it begins:

> Do not let any unwholesome talk come out of your mouths. (4:29)

Any, Paul? How about just a little? How about as long as it's not all the time, it's still okay? **Any**, he says. All of us reading in the 2020s ought to have a sinking feeling in our stomachs. Yet then notice Paul's explanation for why we're to be cautious with our language:

> . . . only what is helpful for building others up according to their needs, that it may benefit those who listen. (4:29b)

The reason for our pure talk is so that the body of Christ will be built up rather than torn down. Paul is relentless in his insistence that our vertical relationship with God must manifest itself in our horizontal relationships with God's people. He has no use for those who love Jesus but hate everyone else.

Paul reinforces the vertical/horizontal dimension again in 4:30: "And do not grieve the Holy Spirit of God, with whom you were sealed for the day of redemption." You might wonder, *"How do you grieve the Holy Spirit?"* Is it when you don't raise hands in worship? Possibly. Is it when you refuse to exercise your spiritual gifts, such as healing or praying in tongues? Maybe. Yet in understanding this question, I am struck by how these words are sandwiched in between more horizontal commands. Check out 4:31: "Get rid of all bitterness, rage and anger, brawling and slander, along with every form of malice." Now, that's some serious instruction, and it puts the "sandwich" of grieving the Holy Spirit in a whole new light. Here's what I mean:

4:29—Use your words to build up.
4:30—*Don't grieve the Holy Spirit.*
4:31—Get rid of bitterness, rage, anger, and the rest.

So, in context, then, we grieve the Holy Spirit when we bring discord to the body of Christ. We grieve the Holy Spirit when our vertical relationship with Jesus does not influence our horizontal relationship with his people. Every time we're tempted to take Paul's commands with a grain of salt, he returns us to the muck and mire of life together in the church community.

We may also be startled at the kind of language Paul uses in 4:31. After all, who in church land would ever be tempted to have "bitterness, rage and anger, brawling and slander, along with every form of malice"? Brawling? Really? Is such a thing possible? Well, a couple of answers there. First, brawling is, of course, possible in church, including physical, verbal, and even legal. I've seen it all. Yet the other factor to remember is that in North American church life, we value "polite." We emphasize "nice." We strive to be "kind." Much of that is possible because of the relative affluence of the culture in which we reside. Not so in the ancient world in general and Ephesus in particular. It was a subsistence economy, with every day's food and shelter involving at least some uncertainty. Subsistence economies have built-in tension and stress, as any trip to the developing world will tell you.

I have noticed one thing about bitterness and rage: many of us love it. We wouldn't feel whole if we didn't have our anger to nurse each day. We're not settled in unless we're stirred up. Is that you? Do you *like* being angry? If your anger were taken away, would you have anything meaningful to replace it with? Are you friends with certain people because you hate the same people? I honestly answer yes to all of the above.

Notice how Paul contends that "getting rid" of this behavior and these attitudes is well within our power as Spirit-filled believers. For every one of us who acts as if "Well, I have this temper, so I might as well use it," Paul responds with "No you don't. Use the power of the Holy Spirit, who is always at the ready." I suppose we don't grieve the Holy Spirit when we actively depend on God to harness our anger and use it for good.

In 4:32—5:2, Paul connects all his commands with the forgiveness of Christ and the love of Christ. Loved people love people. It always works that way. You can't conjure up love from within. You instead reflect it from beyond. As Jesus pours love into you and over you, you're then empowered to love others.

Here's a confession, and it's perhaps one you share as well: I've seen "love" turned into indulgence so often that I don't really know what to do with these commands. Modern Christians often make love into something sentimental and sappy, or they employ it as license to avoid the hard truths of Scripture. How do you love someone well who is destroying lives? Especially if you're in church leadership, how can you live a love that is always redemptive even if it's not always permissive? Does love have any boundaries at all?

These are hard questions, to be sure, but ones that Paul might just address in Ephesians 5:3–20, which is where we're headed next.

**Biblical love isn't always permissive,
but it is always redemptive.**

DAY TWENTY-THREE
Ephesians 5:3-20

The world beckons, calls, and tempts. Whatever it gets from you—your money, your attention, your integrity—it always wants more. It overpromises and underdelivers.

The Word, on the other hand, invites, suggests, and empowers. It gives to you more than it gets from you—hope, purpose, and serenity. It provides what it promises and then some.

You've made the right decision today digging into the Word. Put the world on pause and soak in the Spirit. I can't wait to show you what I mean.

We finished yesterday's short-but-strong section (Ephesians 4:29—5:2) having received the admonition by Paul to "walk in the way of love" (5:2). I immediately asked: How do we ensure that love is not mere sentimentality? How do we avoid the kind of love that is always permissive but rarely redemptive?

We find the reason for those questions in the opening words of the next section: "But among you there must not even be a hint of sexual immorality, or of any kind of impurity, or of greed" (5:3). Well, that doesn't sound very loving, does it? It sounds restrictive, punitive, even puritanical! Until you realize it's beautiful.

Please see what Paul has done here. He has invited the Ephesians to live a life of love in their horizontal relationships—loved people love people—and then immediately placed boundaries around it. He wants to ensure that in this congregation "love of people" doesn't become license to sin. Just because you love someone doesn't mean you endorse or affirm or enable their choices. In fact, in many cases you love people too much to let them continue doing those things that will ultimately destroy them. And when you bring sexual restraint into the conversation in twenty-first-century America, you're immediately accused of being "unloving." The question could even become, "Why don't you make as big a deal of greed? That's in the same verse, after all!"

The answer? No one is trying to turn greed from a sin into a sacrament. No one redefines greed in a way that it becomes the central point of someone's very identity. This only happens with sex and intimacy.

We're in the middle of a highly effective redefinition of the purpose of sex, the body, and marriage in a way that makes men and women the gods and goddesses of their own lives. It's the oldest form of idolatry there is. It's true of how people are treating heterosexual relationships outside of marriage, pornography, and, of course, what the church is to teach and believe regarding same-sex intimacy and romance.

Judging by the flow of Paul's argument, I have to believe that the most loving thing a church can do is teach the beauty of God's design for sexual intimacy, which is celibacy in singleness and faithfulness in heterosexual marriage, in a way that is both gentle and uncompromising. It's less what we're against and more what we're for. At our church in Charlotte, North Carolina, we have many folks – gay and straight – who have surrendered their sexual impulses to God rather than surrendering to them. As others within the congregation make different moral choices, our pastoral stance remains both positive and loving. It's an extraordinarily difficult tightrope we walk – it would be easier to alter what we teach or teach with venom – but, by and large, we have had both impact and grace.

The stakes are high, friends. Paul tells us as much in 5:5: "No immoral, impure or greedy person—such a person is an idolater—has any inheritance in the kingdom of Christ and of God." We don't need to water the gospel down. Instead, we have the privilege of heating it up.

I've said this before but believe it fits now as well: when the church modifies the Word to satisfy the world, it doesn't win more converts. It just earns more contempt.

This teaching is odd, strange, and out of step. I guess that's why I believe it passionately.

Ephesians 5:8 leaps out as well:

> For you were once darkness, but now you are light in the Lord.

Notice the indicative tense. This is what Jesus has accomplished for you and in you. It's not about trying harder but is about trusting more.

From there, Paul spends 5:9–17 encouraging his readers to live careful lives, avoiding proximity to the kinds of sins he listed back in 5:3–5. It's wise to recognize what temptations overpower you, and in response, not to locate yourself near them in the first place. It's why husbands and wives must (yes, I said "must") have each other's cell phone passwords, and why wise families have filters on their internet access.

Paul concludes his extended riff with one of my favorite couplets in verses 5:18–19:

> Do not get drunk on wine, which leads to debauchery. Instead, be filled with the Spirit, speaking to one another with psalms, hymns, and songs from the Spirit.

The first part, regarding wine—or beer or rum or Jack Daniels—is self-evident. The next phrase is genius—"be filled with the Spirit"—for the verb tense there in the original language implies an ongoing filling of the Spirit. It's not as if you can invite God to fill you with the Holy Spirit and then check off that box as "done" in your life. It's a daily, even hourly request, one that we're to make with the utmost urgency.

At last, Paul gives us one of the ways this Spirit-filling happens: "speaking to one another with psalms, hymns, and songs from the Spirit." When we gather and sing, we sing to one another as much as to the Lord himself. Spirit-filling happens much more in community than it ever does in isolation. God will have the last word, and the Spirit does show the winning way.

So today we've gone from sex to Spirit. I wonder what even more troublesome areas we can get into as we near the conclusion of Paul's Ephesian letter . . .

When the church modifies the Word to satisfy the world, it doesn't win more converts; it only earns more contempt.

DAY TWENTY-FOUR
Ephesians 5:21-33

....

Ephesians 5:21–33 is one of *those* passages that people on the outside of the church use to hurl accusations at those within it—that we're backward, Neanderthal, chauvinistic, misogynistic, that we're filled with halitosis, and even that we have dogs and cats living together—mass hysteria!

It's also a passage that people on the inside of the church interpret through all kinds of mental gymnastics as they declare that it (a) doesn't say what it says or (b) says more than what it says.

In contrast to all that, let's see what Paul actually says. Why read *between the lines* when what we read within the lines themselves is pretty spectacular?

To do that, let's revisit one of our favorite literary structures in Scripture: *particularization.* In particularization, an author begins with a general statement and then elaborates on the meaning of that statement with particular examples and instructions.

The troubled history of Ephesians 5 all stems from the fact that interpreters through the years have ignored particularization and instead ripped some verses out of context for use as weapons against women on the one hand and against the church on the other. What is the general statement in Ephesians 5 that the rest of the passage then spells out? Here it is:

Submit to one another out of reverence for Christ. (5:21)

Got that? Writing to a coed church, understanding that it will be read or even performed out loud to a church full of Jews, Gentiles, men, and women, Paul makes a revolutionary declaration: "Submit to one another out of reverence for Christ." Every Jew in the audience would have thought, *I am not submitting to a Gentile.* Every Gentile would have reflected, *I am not submitting to a Jew.* Every husband would have resisted: "I will not submit to my wife." And, yes, every wife would have responded with, "I refuse to submit to my husband." In a world defined by rivalry and competition, and in a culture in which women were property and marriages were based on convenience and commerce, this verse is among the most revolutionary and objectionable of them all.

It's also the verse that we often ignore as we leap immediately to the culturally incendiary words of verse 5:22: "Wives, submit yourselves to your own husbands as you to do the Lord." Before you accuse Paul of what we in the modern world call "hate speech," remember each wife is submitting to a man who has just been told to submit to her as well! Context really is everything.

Paul goes on in verses 23–24 to provide some explanation for how and why wives submit. He roots it in "headship" and bases it in the relationship of Jesus and his church. These words are why, in premarital counseling, I often tell the man that his role in the marriage is to be the spiritual thermostat for the family. He is not the thermometer, which merely reflects the spiritual temperature of the home, but instead the thermostat, which sets it. It is very difficult for a family to advance its own spiritual life beyond that of the father/husband. That is simply the way God has designed our homes to function. You've likely seen examples where this isn't the case—and maybe you are living it right now. Well, God bless every woman who has filled the void left by a husband who couldn't or didn't take this role. My great prayer is that more and more men will discard "thermometering" and embrace "thermostating." Then they'll be obeying Ephesians 5.

Speaking of obeying Ephesians 5, look where Paul goes next in verse 25: "Husbands, love your wives, just as Christ loved the church and gave himself up for her." Many of us have heard these words just enough that we fail to see their power. Paul writes these words to men living in a culture in which women were property and marriage was disposable. *Love my wife?* they'd think. *No, I own her. She's mine.* Paul's answer: "No you don't. God does. Love her well." The gospel is here extraordinarily subversive to the culture in which the church originally proclaimed it. The wives who heard these words in the Ephesian church were simultaneously liberated and delighted.

How did Christ love the church? By becoming its slave. That puts a decidedly different light on "wives, submit to your husbands." When it's "wives, place yourselves under the leadership of a man who is already your servant," you can see how Ephesians 5 brims with the light of Jesus.

Look at the analogy that Paul draws in Ephesians 5:26–31: the marriage relationship between a man and a woman puts the relationship of Jesus and his church on display. "This is a profound mystery," Paul writes (5:32). Nevertheless, it shows us yet again why every marriage is about more than just the two parties involved. Every marriage between believers is a living, breathing testimony to Jesus. What a privilege and a responsibility.

Finally, Paul concludes this section with these words in 5:33: "However, each one of you also must love his wife as he loves himself, and the wife must respect her husband." Love. Respect. That dynamic has come under some undeserved criticism in recent years, but I believe Paul is still spot-on. You'd expect that Paul would end 5:33 with "and the wife must love her husband as well." But he knows something about the human spirit in general and the male psyche in particular. It's this, in the most general of terms:

The most precious words a wife can hear from her husband: "I love you."

The most precious words a husband can hear from his wife: "I'm proud of you."

Love and respect. If you're married, see what these two do for you.

....

For married people, the best way to stay in love is to share a love for the Highest Love.

....

DAY TWENTY-FIVE
Ephesians 6:1-9

Ephesians 5:21–6:9 comes under the heading "Instructions for Christian Households" within the letter. Yesterday the focus was on husbands and wives, and today's emphasis is on parents and children and, yes, slaves and masters.

As we look at 6:1–4, remember how this letter was received in the Ephesian church. It was read out loud, perhaps even with elements of drama and performance, to the gathered church community. They were reading the room as they read the letter. Most of the congregation was likely illiterate. I suspect that the congregation included a large number of families with children, most of whom were at mom and dad's side during the proceedings.

All of a sudden, the reading comes to 6:1: "Children, obey your parents in the Lord, for this is right." And the child moves from distracted to dialed in: "Hey! He's talking to me!" Note that Paul then quotes from the Ten Commandments to reinforce his instruction: "'Honor your father and mother'—which is the first commandment with a promise" (6:2). He either assumes this mostly Gentile congregation has heard of this command or he taught it to them himself. Paul employed this same tactic in 5:31, quoting from Genesis 2 as he taught the Ephesian church about marriage.

At this stage of the public reading of Ephesians, every parent is nodding confidently with the content. Perhaps they're even elbowing their children: "Listen and listen well, son!" Then Paul pulls a most unexpected twist:

> Fathers, do not exasperate your children; instead bring them up in the training and instruction of the Lord. (6:4)

Instantly, the dynamic in the room shifts. Doodling child looks up at "called out" Dad and elbows him: "See, Dad? There's some things you need to hear, too!" And so he does. Paul's words are un-usual in the ancient world, which tended to treat children more as property to be managed than souls to be developed. Notice where Paul expects the children to be trained up in faith: the home. Not the church. He doesn't say, "Bring them to church and they'll take care of your kids' spiritual life for you!" Not at all. It's instead: "The church will come alongside, but you are the primary spiritual influence in the life of your child." It's why we believe that a living relationship with Jesus Christ includes the truth that "faith starts at home."

The letter then turns at 6:5: "Slaves, obey your earthly masters with respect and fear, and with sincerity of heart, just as you would obey Christ." Why address slaves directly? Because they were in the room, hearing this letter being read out loud! As many as 50 percent of the Roman Empire were in fact slaves. You read that right. Slavery was assumed. Challenging it as an institution was not in Paul's realm of thought. Slavery was based on economics, not race, and was not a lifetime sentence. If you want to know how Paul genuinely feels about the whole business, check out 1 Timothy 1:10. If you want to hear God's heart on the matter, read the book of Exodus. Not a verse. The book. A book in which God's heart beats for the freedom of God's people.

Back to Ephesians 6: we're *reading the room* as we're *reading the letter*. In 6:6–8, Paul appeals to the spiritual nature of the slaves hearing his letter. The room likely includes some slave owners who are glancing at their slaves with the implication, "Listen to this, and when we get back home, we've got some work to do." Yet Paul concludes the paragraph with a startling and subversive claim: "You know that the Lord will reward each one for whatever good they do, whether they are slave or free." Do you see what he has done? He first affirmed the personhood of the slaves he's addressing. That was shocking! Then he affirmed that the slaves are on equal footing with their masters in the eyes of the Lord. That was more shocking! Now the slaves are glancing back at their masters and saying, "Are you listening to this?"

The shock continues in 6:9, where Paul addresses masters directly:

> Masters, treat your slaves in the same way. Do not threaten them, since you know that he who is both their Master and yours is in heaven, and there is no favoritism with him.

Game, set, match. The unity that Paul has emphasized from Ephesians 1—a unity we thought only applied to Jews and Gentiles—has now been extended to slaves and masters. Why? Because we're equal in God's sight. From our perspective, think of it this way: one day rocket-flying billionaire Princeton grad Jeff Bezos will die. On that same day so will a villager from India who has survived by begging. At that moment, everything the world values will be stripped away and the one question that these two will have in common will be, "What did you do with Jesus?"

How will you answer that? Regardless of your position in your house, how will you answer this question of questions?

Jesus shed his blood for each person equally.

DAY TWENTY-SIX
Ephesians 6:10-24

....

Paul began the marvel we have as Ephesians with a performance rooted in pronouns. How will he bring it to a close?

Well, it would be nice if he bookended his way to a conclusion that mirrored the opening. Yet he does not. Instead, we see that Paul finishes the letter to the Ephesians in a much different way than he began it.

The metaphor? Paul reveals it in 6:10–11:

> Finally, be strong in the Lord and in his might power. Put on the full armor of God.

In case we missed it, 6:13 gives a reminder: "Therefore, put on the full armor of God."

What has come between 6:11 and 6:13? Paul provides a chilling description of the true nature of the battle in which all of us are involved: "For our struggle is not against flesh and blood, but against the rulers, against the authorities, against the powers of this dark world and against the spiritual forces of evil in the heavenly realms." Satan and his legions are arrayed against the people of God, fostering disunity and weakness at every opportunity. We don't want to see a devil around every corner—nor do we want to blame him for predicaments we got into with no assistance at all—but we don't want to minimize his relentless effort, either.

Our defense, again, is this full armor of God.

Here's how Paul breaks it down (or, particularizes it, if you remember some of the literary structures we've been talking about):

the belt of truth
the gospel of peace fitting your feet

the shield of faith
the helmet of salvation
the sword of the Spirit

Maybe you have sat through lengthy five-point sermons that dealt with each of those in succession. Yet I wonder if pressing each of the different pieces of the armor for details almost misses the point, which is that we are under attack. Soldiers don't fight battles alone, and the entire "army" of the church needs to be prepared and growing in and toward maturity. You'll only overcome Satan's efforts if you're grounded in your salvation and growing in your knowledge of and dependence upon the Word. Really, you can make the case that what you're doing right now is a form of "putting on" the full armor of God so that you might embrace this day rather than be overwhelmed by it.

As Paul gets to verse 18, he moves off the metaphor and into closing instructions.

And pray in the Spirit on all occasions with all kinds of prayers and requests.

What is "praying in the Spirit"? You may want to check out 1 Corinthians 14 (the whole chapter) to get a glimpse of at least part of what that means.

Paul invites prayers for himself as well: "Pray also for me" (Ephesians 6:19). Look at the content of Paul's prayer request: "that whenever I speak, words may be given me so that I will fearlessly make known the mystery of the gospel" (6:19). The phrase "words may be given me" is one of the most liberating in Scripture, particularly for those who proclaim and teach the Word. We don't have to invent the words; we inherit them. We don't buy them from an expert; they've been given to us by the Savior. Some of my most rewarding prayers are with my hands hovering over a keyboard, asking that God would give me more compelling and impactful words than I could ever conjure up on my own.

Ephesians 6:21–22 gives you a window into how New Testament letters traveled. Tychicus is apparently Paul's version of Amazon Prime, delivering this letter to the Ephesian church with record speed. He had the same job in Colossians 4:7. Tychicus delivers not only parchment but also spiritual sustenance as well: "that he may encourage you" (Ephesians 6:22).

Paul concludes with a blessing of "peace" (6:23) and "grace" (6:24) to this formerly conflicted but now united congregation. I suspect that those who heard (and saw) the letter read to them have gone through a roller coaster of emotions—from grief to sadness, from guilt to forgiveness, from shame to grace, and from isolation to community.

I mentioned in the introduction to Ephesians that God used this letter to bring me back from the brink. May he use it to bring you to the brink, not of abandoning faith but of coming alive in grace.

The conclusion of Ephesians is a marvelous opportunity to begin a season of prayer for your own spiritual sustenance and that of your congregation.

FIVE CORE CONVICTIONS
of the 'Come Alive' series

O n many occasions in my time in pastoral ministry, I have recommended to people that they "read the Bible" as part of their life with God. Sometimes, in exasperation, I felt like grabbing them by the shoulders, giving a good shake, and imploring, "Just read the Bible, will ya?!"

Except now I know that I was doing little more than giving a tone deaf lecture to the Ethiopian eunuch in Acts 8 who asks plaintively, "How can I ... unless someone explains it to me?"

That realization formed the genesis of the reading guides known as *Come Alive.* Whether it's at the church I serve, Good Shepherd Church in Charlotte, North Carolina, or people following online or reading this book, I have stopped demanding – "Read more!" -- and started empowering – "Here are ways to understand what we're reading together." I no longer want to cajole people into reading the Bible; I want to come alongside and give just enough insight to people so they can understand and delight in the Scripture they do read.

As we enter the biblical world, I come to this joyful task with five core convictions:

1. ***The Bible is not a book, it's a library.*** I cringe when I hear Scripture called "The Good Book" but I come alive when it's named "The Great Library." The biblical library contains sixty-six books written by as many as forty authors over a timespan of more than 1,000 years and in multiple writing styles. Within the biblical library, we have historical narrative, legal directives, songs of faith, words of wisdom, letters from prison to churches in crisis, and even erotic poetry. You interpret each book well when you first determine what genre it represents.

2. *As I heard in seminary, Context Is Everything (C.I.E.).*
Context here has within it at least two meanings. First, we explore the literary context within the books themselves. We can only understand what Matthew says in one part of his Gospel, for example, when we first understand its overall thrust. Even more particularly, we best understand one section within Galatians when we understand those sections that come before it and after it. Second, in addition to the literary context within biblical books, we also understand that the cultural, geographical, and historical context of each author's life will play a tremendously important role in shaping his book. As far as we can, we'll seek to understand the role of place, time, and values in each author's inspired narrative.

3. *Reading "the Bible" is much more interesting than reading "Bible verses."* Biblical books are not merely collections of isolated sayings or spectacular events. They are instead intricate wholes with a purposeful design – the product of the literary and theological genius of each author. We'll spend less time memorizing part and more time understanding the whole.

4. *When people ask, "Do you interpret the Bible 'literally' or 'symbolically,' the correct answer is 'literarily.'"* When we understand that it is a library and not a book (see #1 above), we realize that the first task of any interpreter is to determine the genre of a particular book, or even section within a book, and then understand it accordingly. It's why the interpretive task for the book of Revelation is much different than for Proverbs. Throughout *Come Alive,* we'll see there are many moments within books that are literal, a few that are symbolic, a few more that are subtly comedic, and others that are a combination of all of the above. We'll be interpreting the Bible literarily.

5. *God-breathed is more alive than God-dictated ever could be.* We believe with St. Paul that "all Scripture is God-breathed" (2 Timothy 3:16). What does that mean and how is it different from God-dictated? Well, if the Bible were God-dictated, the authors would be little more than scribes with no

more creativity than robots. God said it, they transcribed it, and we believe it. God-breathed is so much different, more alive, and warmer than that. God-breathed means that God took the personalities of the biblical authors and breathed life and truth into their words without diminishing who they were as men and women. It's why you see so much of Paul's personality, complete with quirks and eccentricities, in his letters to the New Testament churches. It's why you see the thunder of Peter in his letters, the art of David in his songs, and even the despair of Solomon in Ecclesiastes.

With those convictions and that understanding, get ready for a daily journey into the biblical text. We're not speed reading through the Word of God; we're savoring a small morsel each day, knowing that we'll be different at the end of our trek than we were at its beginning.